OVERCOMING DEPRESSION ONE STEP AT A TIME

THE NEW BEHAVIORAL ACTIVATION APPROACH TO GETTING YOUR LIFE BACK

MICHAEL E. ADDIS, PH.D.

CHRISTOPHER R. MARTELL, PH.D., ABPP

New Harbinger Publications, Inc.

Distributed in Canada by Raincoast Books

Copyright © 2004 by Michael E. Addis and Christopher R. Martell
New Harbinger Publications, Inc.
5674 Shattuck Avenue
Oakland, CA 94609

Cover design by Amy Shoup
Acquired by Catharine Sutker
Edited by Brady Kahn
Text design by Tracy Marie Carlson

ISBN-10 1-57224-367-8
ISBN-13 978-1-57224-367-5

Printed in the United States of America

New Harbinger Publications' website address: www.newharbinger.com

15 14 13

20 19 18 17 16 15 14 13

Contents

Part 3
Activation as an Approach to Your Daily Life

Introduction

If you are considering reading this book, it is likely that you or someone you love is experiencing a period of depression. This book will take you through a process of working your way out of depression. Over the past seven years, the authors of this workbook have worked as a clinical supervisor and a therapist on a major research project funded by the National Institute of Mental Health. This research revealed that a form of therapy known as *behavioral activation* is effective in helping people recover from depression. Behavioral activation, or *self-activation*, is a technique designed to help you develop a plan to take small steps toward reengaging in your life. Many people seem to shut down when they are depressed. Self-activation helps you to better understand how your actions from day to day, even moment to moment, have an effect on your mood. Once you understand how this works, you can begin to make strategic changes in your actions that will help you end depression and build a better life.

THE PURPOSE OF THIS WORKBOOK

There are several self-help books available to people who are trying to cope with depression. Why, then, have we written another one? The short story is that this book represents a new direction. The approach described in this workbook has been shown in two large controlled research studies to be an effective strategy for ending depression (Dimidjian et al. 2003; Jacobson et al. 1996). Up till now, there has been no guide available to help people use this approach themselves.

Self-activation has actually been used in the treatment of depression for decades. Therapists from a variety of schools of thought have recognized the importance of helping depressed people get reengaged in their lives. While some therapies use an activation approach only as a first step, however, we use it as the solution to getting out of depression. And whereas other self-help books or workbooks on depression may briefly discuss activation, this book focuses exclusively on this approach. As you will see, there's a lot more to self-activation than "getting active." This workbook will show you how to identify the particular areas in your life that need work and how to determine the specific changes that will help to end your depression.

Can Talk Therapies and Workbooks Really Help?

Treatments for depression vary widely. Medications are increasingly common, and several different types of psychotherapy have been shown to help people recover from depression. Recent scientific understanding is clear: talk therapies alone (psychotherapy, behavior therapy, counseling) can be effective in helping people recover from depression and in preventing relapse (Seligman 1995). Talk therapies can also be helpful in combination with medication (Elkin et al. 1989). Medication alone is effective in recovery, but people frequently relapse unless they stay on their medication. On the other hand, there is some evidence that talk therapies are more effective than medication in preventing relapse (Hollon, Shelton, and Loosen 1991). In addition, several studies have shown that *bibliotherapy* (a fancy word for reading self-help material on depression) by itself can be an effective treatment (Scogin et al. 1990).

It is important not only to understand depression but also to develop a plan of action for coping with your depression and ending its harmful effects. This workbook will help you do that. By following the step-by-step program outlined here, you will better understand the nature of depression and, more importantly, begin taking steps to feel better and accomplish more in your life. You can use the exercises in this workbook on your own time and at your own pace. We understand that when you are depressed you may have difficulty doing even the smallest tasks. This workbook breaks down the task of getting reengaged and active into smaller tasks. You've taken the first step by purchasing this book, which was a relatively easy step. All of the exercises in this book can be seen as equally small steps leading toward the larger goal of getting your life back on track.

How to Use This Book

This is the beginning of your process, and you should take your time with the workbook. Spend at least a week on each chapter. The goal of this book is to provide you with tools that you will use repeatedly to overcome depression. Pace yourself. If you complete the reading and exercises in each chapter weekly, this process should take you at least eight weeks. Most of the exercises in this book can be repeated. Many of them may not relate directly to your situation, but you should complete them anyway for practice. It will be useful to photocopy some of the exercises so that you can do them multiple times. The book is planned to be used in sequence and to serve as a future resource for you. The first time you read it through and complete the exercises, do them in the order written. Thereafter, you can skip around to reread only the chapters that you find most helpful.

DEPRESSION AND THE WORLD WE LIVE IN

People become depressed for a variety of reasons. In the United States alone, roughly 25 percent of the population will experience serious depression at some point in their lives. Furthermore, research has shown that if you have been depressed once you are likely to have a second episode of depression or to become chronically depressed. Biological explanations for depression are not sufficient to account for the vast increase in cases of depression over the past fifty years; the incidence has tripled since World War II. Another explanation is the greater sophistication of the mental-health community in its ability to diagnose depression. People used to take to their beds because of a "nervous breakdown," but this label was too vague to be useful. Psychologists, psychiatrists, and other behavioral health specialists can now specify with greater clarity the types of problems people experience and provide diagnostic labels that help in the development of treatment plans.

Contextual Change: When Too Many Changes Lead to Depression

It has also been suggested that the growing number of depressed people can be attributed to a "depressogenic society," a society that places many of its members at risk for developing depression. In this global economy, a World Wide Web of Internet connections is available at the touch of your fingertips, but people have become increasingly isolated and alienated. The conveniences of modern life allow people to rely less on one another and more on technology. In Western societies, the nuclear family (mom, dad—perhaps—and the kids) is commonplace. Extended families, including uncles, aunts, grandparents, and even great-grandparents, living in the same household or in the same neighborhood is much less common. Adults often live thousands of miles from the cities and towns of their birth and from their families of origin. Corporate culture has turned individuals into "human resources"—chess pieces on a board with positions that are frequently eliminated to maintain a financial bottom line. Is it any wonder that more people feel lethargic, pessimistic, and hopeless in their lives?

All of these factors account for the increase in depression over the last fifty years. *Contexual change* is the term psychologists use to describe an increase in situations that put people at risk for depression. The situations, or contexts, in which people live have shifted radically. Human beings are adaptable, but sometimes the world changes, and people may be able to advance technologically at a quicker rate than they can cope psychologically.

In addition to contextual changes at a societal level, many people experience contextual changes in their personal lives. They begin and end relationships, change jobs, lose jobs, lose loved ones, move to new homes, or more gradually begin to change the way they approach life. Research has shown that these sorts of life changes can also place you at risk for depression.

Exercise: Recognizing Your Contextual Change

List below the changes that have taken place in your life over the past six months. Changes can be great or small and you can experience them as positive or negative. You may have had a promotion at work (a large positive change), or you may have been laid off (a large negative change); you might have remodeled a room in your house (a small positive change), or you may have gotten shorted by a few dollars on a paycheck for one pay period (a small negative change).

_____

_____

_____

_____

_____

_____

A WORKBOOK FOR SELF-ACTIVATION

No workbook can provide solutions to all of the potential societal and personal problems that can lead to depression. But this workbook can, and does, provide effective ways to enhance your understanding of how depression works in your life and strategies to make the sorts of changes necessary to end depression.

Self-activation is a process of guided activity. If you are using this workbook in conjunction with psychotherapy, you will have the guidance of a therapist to help you in your activation process. You can also use this workbook on your own. Doing the exercises will help you learn habits that will allow you to cope better with your life, depressed or not. Research has shown that the techniques described here can effectively end depression and help prevent it from returning in the future. So don't wait. There is no time like the present to begin regaining control of your life.

Part I

Understanding Depression

Chapter 1

How Depression Works

Several years ago, Randall finished graduate school, got married, and moved across the country to start a new job. In many ways, Randall had worked most of his adult life to reach this point. It was a very exciting time with lots of possibilities. Within a few weeks of arriving at his new home, however, Randall began to notice a certain sadness creeping over him. He had always enjoyed hiking, listening to music, and reading, but now these activities held little interest for him. After feeling this way for a couple of weeks, he began to have trouble falling asleep and began waking several times during the night. As a result, he had difficulty concentrating at work or at home. This led to persistent feelings of guilt about not being more productive at his new job and a general feeling of hopelessness that things could ever improve.

What happened that turned an otherwise joyful time of life into such a consistent downer? Of course, you may recognize that Randall was experiencing depression. But naming a problem is only a starting point. The real question is, how do people successfully end depression? Answering this question is what this book is all about.

TOP TEN DEPRESSION QUESTIONS

When Randall started noticing that he was depressed, he began to ask himself a series of questions. Some of the particular questions he asked are common ones when people experience depression. Here are the top ten:

1. "What's wrong with me?"

2. "What's causing me to feel this way?"

3. "Am I a failure for feeling this way?"

4. "Am I depressed because of a personal weakness?"

5. "Do I have some kind of chemical imbalance?"

6. "Is there something in my childhood or past that's making me feel this way?"

7. "How can I overcome this?"

8. "Should I take medication?"

9. "Do other people feel this way?"

10. "Will I ever be able to feel 'normal'?"

Exercise: Reviewing Your Depression Questions

Take a look at the list of questions above and think about how many of them you ask yourself and how often. A good portion of them may seem familiar to you. If some of them seem particularly familiar, circle the numbers or put a star next to them. These are questions that concern you, and it will be helpful to refer back to them as you progress through the workbook.

This workbook will address some of these questions in future chapters. For now, here are some brief answers:

1. What's wrong with you?

Nothing is wrong with you. There are reasons that you're depressed that have to do with your life. We'll have much more to say about this.

2. What's causing you to feel this way?

Complex experiences like depression rarely have one cause. Research shows that it often isn't necessary to determine an exact cause in order to end depression.

3. Are you a failure for feeling this way?

Absolutely not. People do not choose to feel depressed. However, you may choose to act in ways that can make your depression worse or in ways that will make you feel better.

4. Are you depressed because of a personal weakness?

This is similar to the last question and our answer is the same. No.

5. Do you have some kind of chemical imbalance?

Some research shows a relationship between the amount of certain chemicals in the nervous system and the likelihood of being depressed. However, it's not clear whether the biochemical process causes depression or the depression causes a change in the biochemical process. Contrary to conventional thinking—that some form of chemical imbalance makes you feel or act depressed—it is possible that feeling and acting depressed may alter the level of certain chemicals in your brain.

6. Is there something in your childhood or past that's making you feel this way?

For some people, experiences in childhood can increase the likelihood of developing depression as an adult. Nonetheless, the quickest way to remove the effects of the past is to approach life differently in the present.

7. How can you overcome this?

There are a variety of effective treatments for depression that have been tested in controlled research studies. This workbook's approach is based on the idea of behavioral activation, which is really a technical way of saying "getting engaged in your life."

8. Should you take medication?

Certain medications have been shown to be effective for depression. However, as with all treatments, some people benefit from taking medication, and some don't. Even if you think that depression is strictly a medical illness, there are effective ways to overcome it that don't involve medication. If you think you might want to try taking medication, you should consult with your primary care physician or a psychiatrist.

9. Do other people feel this way?

Yes. One out of ten people experience an episode of serious depression every year. One out of four will experience an episode in their lifetime.

10. Will you ever be able to feel "normal"?

You will certainly be able to feel less depressed, more energized, more engaged in your life, and less down. We're not sure what "normal" means, since life is an emotional process; lots of things happen and you are, in many ways, blessed to be able to have strong feelings in your life.

Exercise: Reviewing the Answers

Now look over the above list of answers to each question. Place a star next to the answers that sound right to you or make you feel more hopeful about ending depression. Place a question mark next to the answers that either don't convince you or aren't clear. If you're working with a therapist, you might want to discuss your thoughts about these questions and answers to help you clarify how you understand your depression.

Checkpoint

Are any of the answers to the top ten depression questions different from what you expected?

Yes _____ No _____

WHAT IS DEPRESSION?

If you look at the questions and answers above, you'll notice that it's common to think of depression as something "inside" yourself. You may think depression is something biological, like a chemical imbalance, or something psychological, like poor self-esteem or negative thoughts or beliefs. Either way, when people become depressed, it is typically themselves they look at first. Often, what they see looks pretty dim. This isn't too surprising because, of course, when you're depressed you tend to see the bad rather than the good.

Our belief is that depression does not live inside a person, no matter how much it feels that way. Depression is a problem between you and your life, rather than a problem inside of you. Unfortunately, when you become depressed, it can be very hard to focus on anything except what's wrong inside. Consider the following conversation Randall had with a friend, Sarah, several weeks after moving across the country:

Sarah: Wow, you've got a lot going on. It sounds stressful.

Randall: Yes I do. But it's all positive stuff. New job, new family, new place to live. I've been working toward this for a long time. Why can't I enjoy it and relax like everyone else seems to be able to?

Sarah: I doubt everyone else is as happy in situations like this as you think.

Randall: That's probably true, but it still feels wrong.

Sarah: Well, you've been through a lot of changes. What do you do with yourself when you feel so down?

Randall: I mostly sit in my office and try to figure out why I'm feeling this way. I'm a psychologist. I should be able to figure it out.

Sarah: Does it help to think a lot about why you're depressed?

Randall: Probably not.

Sarah made two crucial points in this conversation. First, she pointed out that there are reasons why Randall would be feeling depressed. He left his home, started a new challenging job, moved with his wife across the country where they knew no one, and so on. Second, Sarah focused on how Randall was responding to feeling depressed and how it was working for him. Were Randall's attempts to cope with depression helping or making the situation worse?

Ending Depression: The Steps You Need to Take

Here is a preview of the steps to ending depression that this workbook will cover.

Step 1. Understand how depression works, particularly the links between what you do, where you do it, how you do it, and how it makes you feel.

Step 2. Identify particular areas of life where the way you're responding to depression isn't helping and learn how to change the response.

Step 3. Learn to approach difficult situations rather than avoid them.

Step 4. Begin to address larger life issues that may put you at risk for developing another episode of depression.

Exercise: Examining the Steps

The four steps above describe, in a general way, the self-activation approach to ending depression. How do they strike you? You might consider jotting down some notes or thoughts about each step. Do they make you more optimistic? Skeptical?

_____

_____

_____

_____

_____

If this approach seems simple to you, it both is and isn't. Although the basic ideas are very straightforward, applying them to your particular situation requires you to be a bit of a scientist. You'll need to think carefully and creatively, and also be willing to try some experiments to see what happens. This workbook is designed to guide you through this process. But before going any further, it's worth taking some time to consider how depression works.

HOW DEPRESSION OPERATES

Depression is often described as an illness with at least five of the following symptoms. At least one of them must be symptom number 1 or 2 (American Psychiatric Association, 1994):

1. sadness or depressed mood

2. loss of interest or pleasure in all or most things that you usually enjoy

3. significant weight loss or gain

4. difficulty sleeping (too much or too little sleep)

5. feeling very restless (unable to sit still) or feeling very slowed down

6. being tired all the time

7. having feelings of worthlessness or guilt

8. difficulty thinking or concentrating

9. having repeated thoughts of death or dying

These symptoms need to be present for a period of at least two weeks and occur most of the day nearly every day. Furthermore, you must rule out other factors such as medical illness or the effects of drugs, alcohol, or certain medications, which could cause these symptoms.

Exercise: Getting to Know Your Symptoms

Read over the above list of symptoms again and circle or put a star by those that describe your experience. If some symptoms of your depression aren't covered in the list, write them down below and write down how long you have been experiencing them.

1. _____

2. _____

3. _____

4. _____

5. _____

Even if you don't meet the criteria determined by the American Psychiatric Association, you may still benefit from working on depression. Note: If you are experiencing fewer than three of the symptoms we listed, or if you are experiencing neither number 1 nor number 2, you may want to consult with a therapist, a psychiatrist, or your primary care physician. You could be experiencing something other than depression.

Checkpoint

Does depression, according to the definition above, sound like the sort of problem you are experiencing?

Yes _____ No _____

Is Depression an Illness?

Depression is recognized as an identifiable illness by the American Psychiatric Association, and by health-care professionals around the country. Knowing this can help to relieve some of the self-blame and hopelessness that you may feel when you're depressed. This is a good thing. It helps to be optimistic about the future and to see depression as something other than a personal weakness or a character flaw.

The idea that depression is a medical illness also poses some problems however. First, knowing that depression is a set of symptoms doesn't tell you much about how those symptoms came about or how to get rid of them. Second, when you think of a medical illness, you may tend to think of an illness that is caused entirely by physical malfunctions in your body. In fact, most of the research that has been done shows that physical, behavioral, cognitive (thinking), and environmental factors are all potentially important in causing and maintaining depression. Lack of social support from friends or family, stressful life events, negative thinking, and relationship difficulties have all been shown to be associated with depression.

Third, and perhaps most importantly, when you think of a medical illness, you may often assume that only medical treatments can be helpful. People often say things like, "If my depression is caused by a chemical imbalance, then how could anything but medication help me?" In fact, as we said above, many nonbiological factors may cause or maintain depression.

So if depression is not strictly a medical illness, what is it? This is a little bit like asking, "What is love?" Just like love, depression refers to a complex set of human experiences. This is why many psychologists and researchers think of depression as a biological-psychological-environmental process. In plain English, depression is like a very complex sauce. Comparing depression to a sauce may seem odd, but bear with us. If you follow the recipe for a particular sauce, you can see all of the individual ingredients. However, no single ingredient alone can account for the taste of the whole sauce, and each ingredient supports the others in some way. If you made a change in any ingredient, the whole sauce itself would taste different. Depression works the same way. Each ingredient, including the biological, the behavioral, the cognitive, and the interpersonal, works together. You may strongly believe that only one ingredient contributes to your depression. For example, many people believe that their depression is clearly caused by a chemical imbalance because it feels so innate. Nevertheless, changing what you do will have an impact on this biological process. Just like taking an antidepressant may make it easier to find energy to complete tasks, completing tasks and getting active can effect changes in your brain.

Keep in mind that diagnoses such as "depression" are culturally specific. People at different times in history or in different cultures may not experience depression in the same way that Westerners experience it today. Although it is clear that people throughout history have most likely had broken bones, bruises, and upset stomachs, it is less clear whether they experienced their psychological world in the same way that people do today. This points again to the fact that depression is a complex problem, and that you may be living in a society that makes you more prone to depression on a number of levels. It is a relief to know, however, that you can deal with this complex problem through relatively simple means. The approach described in this workbook may be the one that will work for you.

The Depression Loop

Many researchers and mental-health professionals have observed that depression operates as a cycle, or a feedback loop. In other words, things in life can lead you to be depressed and depression can make those same things worse. The loop goes on and on. Consider how it operates in the life of a client named Karrie.

Karrie is a thirty-seven-year old high school teacher who recently became depressed following the loss of her job. Cutbacks in education funding at the state level had led to many layoffs, so Karrie knew she wasn't the only one. Still, she often wonders why this happened to her and what she did to cause it. At times, she can spend hours staring at the television thinking about the things going wrong in her life. Before she became depressed, Karrie enjoyed socializing with friends, exercising, reading, and going to movies. Now she has little interest in these activities. The more depressed she feels, the less she wants to talk to friends or to even leave the house. The more she sits by herself in her house, the more depressed she feels. As the figure below suggests, Karrie is caught in circular trap or feedback loop.

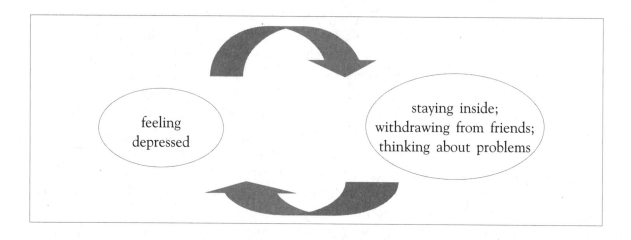

The idea of a loop or cycle helps to explain why depression can be so difficult to end without help. If we asked Karrie what she's doing instead of socializing and exercising, she would probably say she's trying to feel better. When you're depressed, it often feels better (in the short run) to stay at home than it does to go out. This raises another important point about the depression loop: The things you do to try to cope with depression sometimes make it worse. Some things that work in the short run may make depression worse in the long run.

Exercise: What Are Your Coping Attempts?

Write down three or four things you sometimes do to try to cope with feeling blue, fatigued, sleepless, or otherwise depressed. Put a plus sign next to the activity if it makes you feel better in the short run, a minus sign if it makes you feel worse, or a circle if it seems to have a neutral effect.

_____

_____

_____

_____

ENDING DEPRESSION: A PREVIEW OF WHAT'S TO COME

Self-activation makes use of guided activity. Using this workbook as a guide, you can learn to understand your behavioral patterns and replace less-effective strategies with new behaviors. By looking at the effect of new behaviors on your mood or your sense of accomplishment, you will be able to decide if these changes are worthwhile. You will focus on trying new behaviors and observing the outcome. You may be concerned about what it means to focus on new activities and behaviors. You may think that doing so means eating popcorn, jogging, playing cards, or doing other "fun" activities. If you are skeptical about the possibility of ending your depression by focusing on behaviors such as these, it's understandable. The fact is, positive or fun activities don't necessarily change your depression. If just having fun helped, you could probably spend a day at an amusement park and not be depressed. Obviously, it doesn't work this way. Self-activation uses the terms *behavior* and *activity* more broadly.

Virtually everything you do is behavior. For example, as you sit reading this book, you are behaving a certain way. When you stop and think about what you've read, that is another behavior. Lying in bed in the morning is a behavior, as is telling a loved one that you care about them. Also, two behaviors that look the same on the surface may have very different meanings and consequences. Lying in bed on a Saturday morning and enjoying a cup of coffee is a different activity than lying in bed feeling depressed and worrying about work.

When you are depressed, hearing someone encourage you to change your behavior can make you think that you are expected to "just do it." Although the focus of this book is on helping you reengage in your life, the techniques are written with an understanding that change can be difficult, especially when you are depressed. We know that if you could have "just done it" you would have done so long ago.

The remainder of this book describes specific things you can do to end depression. Although later chapters go into greater detail, here's a preview so that you have a sense of where you're going. There is no surefire recipe whereby you can simply combine two teaspoons of exercise and a tablespoon of optimism, mix them up, and live a depression-free life. The critical ingredients vary from person to person. Nonetheless, you can look forward to the following.

Getting to Know Yourself Better

You may have repeatedly heard the advice, "Get to know yourself." You may think of therapy as a process of self-discovery. But what are you getting to know when you discover yourself? This may seem like a strange question, but it raises an important point. When most people think about getting to know themselves, they focus on such things as their feelings, beliefs, values, attitudes, personalities, and so on. All of these things are typically assumed to be inside of you. What people often leave out are the things that are outside, such as how they act around friends and coworkers, how they spend their free time, how they approach tedious tasks, and so forth. These things matter a great deal.

It can be very difficult to change how you feel, your personality, or your values. It's often easier at first to change your activities: what you're doing, where you're doing it, who you're doing it with, and when you're doing it. Changing what you do can have a direct effect on what you feel and think. But before you begin to make specific changes in your activities, you must first become an expert on what you currently do. As you observe your behavior, you will also observe what effect different behaviors in different settings have on your mood. Chapter 2 is devoted entirely to this topic.

Taking Control by Experimenting

Once you have a handle on your activities and the effects they have on your mood, you can begin to try to do some things differently. For example, Karrie observed that her mood tended to get worse when she sat in front of the television and tried to figure out what she had done wrong. Karrie and her therapist designed an experiment to see whether substituting a different activity for a brief amount of time would make even the slightest difference in Karrie's mood. Perhaps it wouldn't, but it was clear to Karrie that what she currently was doing wasn't working.

Rather than watching television, she decided to spend time talking to friends on the phone or writing letters from eight to eight-thirty each evening. Then, she could return to watching television and thinking about why she was laid off. Her therapist emphasized to Karrie that this sort of change would probably not end Karrie's depression. The goal was more modest than that: to see where small changes in Karrie's behavior might shift her mood, even slightly, in a more positive direction. In fact, Karrie found that her mood improved considerably when she was writing or talking to friends, and it got worse when she returned to watching television. Over time, several experiments like this led to the discovery of patterns in Karrie's response to depressed mood. She was ultimately able to identify her typical ways of responding and to substitute alternative ways that had a more positive effect.

Blocking Avoidance

One of the most common ways people try to cope with depression is by avoiding things that make them anxious, sad, stressed, or otherwise uncomfortable. In many ways, this makes perfect sense. If you're already depressed, why make yourself feel worse? Unfortunately, what you are doing in the short run to feel better could be making your depression worse, or it could be preventing you from solving important problems. We have worked with numerous people who cope with depression by avoiding friends and family or putting off important tasks such as updating a resume or paying bills. Although these behaviors often help to reduce anxiety and stress in the short run, it's easy to see how they maintain depression in the long run; they feed right back into the depression loop. Learning to cope with difficult emotions while actively *approaching* particular tasks or situations is a highly effective way of blocking avoidance.

Sometimes what people avoid can be less concrete or obvious. For example, you may be avoiding painful emotions or situations. Endlessly worrying about finances, for example, may help you avoid strong feelings of sadness over the loss of a loved one. Approaching rather than avoiding the feelings would involve experiencing the grief and sadness, perhaps by talking with others about the loss. Often, the more you avoid experiencing negative feelings, the longer the negative feelings remain.

Another example of subtle avoidance that usually doesn't feel like a choice is fatigue. When things are going badly in your life, you may have an overwhelming feeling of fatigue or a need to sleep. There is no obvious connection to events or negative feelings, but you simply feel exhausted. When you are exhausted, you probably sleep. However, problems never go away when you are asleep, they are just on hold.

Dealing with Larger Life Issues and Preventing Depression from Returning

The depression loop is often set in motion by particular events. Sometimes these events are quite sudden and dramatic, such as the loss of a job, the end of a relationship, a move across country, or the loss of a loved one. A great deal of research has shown that these sorts of life events can place you at risk for depression. In other cases, important events are much more subtle, and they unfold over time. For example, you might, over the course of several months or years, begin to work longer and longer hours, while spending less and less time with family and friends. If asked, you probably wouldn't be able to identify any particular event associated with the beginning of depression. However, over the course of time, your life would have changed. These sorts of changes are no less powerful than sudden dramatic changes when it comes to creating a depression loop.

Ending depression doesn't always require dealing with a major life change or making major changes in the future. Nonetheless, you should increase your awareness of and make some changes in your situation if certain issues leave you at risk for developing another episode of depression. Issues vary from person to person. For example, you may find that you need to better maintain strong social and emotional ties to important people in your life. Or you may find that keeping to a relatively structured routine is important. You may need to find a job that better matches your abilities and interests, or you may need to resolve long-standing conflicts with close friends or family members. By studying your behavior-mood links, experimenting with new behaviors and activities, and learning to approach rather than to avoid problems, you will feel more empowered to address the issues in your life that contribute to depression.

YOU'VE GOT QUESTIONS

If you've read this far, you probably have questions about our approach to ending depression. In fact, we hope that you do. The better you understand the approach, and the more you have the sense that it fits for you, the more likely you are to benefit from this workbook. Below are several of the most common questions we have heard from people being introduced to this approach.

What about Genetic or Biological Factors?

There is now little doubt that genetic factors play a role in depression. The scientific evidence on genetics comes from two major findings. First, depression tends to run in families. When an illness is common among family members, it is often assumed to have at least some genetic component, although families share much more than their genes. Second, identical twins raised in separate family environments tend to have related symptoms of depression more often than nonidentical twins who are raised in the same family environment do (Gatz et al. 1992). Because identical twins in these studies share all the same genetic material but not the same family environment, these findings suggest that genetic factors play a role in depression.

Notice the words "play a role." We didn't say "cause" or "are the reason for," because no research has shown that depression is caused specifically by—and only by—genetics. As mentioned before, there is an equally strong body of research pointing to the importance of life events in leading to depression. In addition, many people are able to end depression by changing their behavior, the way they think, or other nongenetic or biological processes. Thus, the approach described here can be helpful regardless of whether depression is ultimately found to have a genetic basis.

What about a Chemical Imbalance?

You may have heard that depression is caused by an imbalance of certain chemicals called "neurotransmitters" in the nervous system. In many ways, the issues here are similar to those involved in genetic or biological explanations for depression. Again, there is ample evidence that depression is correlated with a variety of social, environmental, psychological, and biological factors. "Correlated" means that two things tend to go together, although it isn't clear which one is the cause of the other or whether some other factor is involved. For example, income and education levels are correlated in this country. On average, although there are many exceptions, people who are more highly educated also tend to make more money. But does education cause people to make more money, or does greater wealth lead to a higher likelihood of being educated? Simply knowing that the two are related doesn't answer this question.

The same sort of confusion between correlation and causation applies to depression and neurotransmitters. Do problems with neurotransmitters cause depression, or does depression cause problems with neurotransmitters? Or is there some other factor that causes both? Regardless of what the causes are, research has shown that changing behavior can be a very effective way to end depression. Unfortunately, many people believe that if there is a relationship between something biological and a problem like depression, the only way to effectively treat the problem is with medication. This simply isn't true.

What about the Past?

By now you probably have a pretty good sense that our approach to ending depression focuses on changing behaviors and activities. Where do these behaviors come from? They certainly don't appear out of nowhere. Your past—from your childhood up through your adult life, and on into the present—affects how you behave. You learned that particular behaviors work for particular purposes, while others are less effective. As a result, you developed habits of which you may not even be aware. For example, if you grew up in a family environment with a great deal of anger and conflict, you might have learned to behave very timidly around other people's anger. If someone were to scowl or raise their voice in anger, you might respond by lowering your eyes, not speaking, or engaging in other submissive behaviors. These behaviors may have worked in the past because they tended to keep the anger from being directed at you. You might continue to behave timidly as an adult, even though it causes problems in the long run; for example, you could be passed over for a promotion because you lacked assertiveness.

Thus, your past is extremely important in shaping who you are now. However, as we suggested above, the quickest way to remove the effect of the past is to begin to act differently. According to this approach, change does not require that you develop complete insight into the workings of your childhood but only that you begin to learn new ways of being an adult.

Exercise: What Habits Did You Develop While Growing Up?

Part 1. Listed below are some experiences that you may recall from the past. This list is offered to help you begin to take educated guesses about the types of habits you may have developed long ago that are now influencing your depression. Circle the experiences that tended to be true for you as you were growing up.

1. How people expressed emotions in your family:

    ♦ They never displayed them.

    ♦ They showed emotions in violent or dramatic ways.

    ♦ They expressed emotions tenderly.

2. How authorities disciplined you:

    ♦ They punished you inconsistently.

    ♦ They punished you whether you were behaving well or badly.

    ♦ They never punished you; they let you do what you wanted.

    ♦ They talked rationally to you, explaining the consequences of your behavior.

    ♦ They applied consistent, loving discipline.

3. How you knew you were loved and cared for:

    ♦ You were often told that you were loved.

- ♦ You were hugged, kissed, and cuddled in loving, appropriate ways.

- ♦ You did not know you were loved; nobody showed love or affection.

4. How you reacted to other people:

- ♦ You were shy and reserved and rarely approached others.

- ♦ You interacted with people that you trusted but were shy around strangers.

- ♦ You were polite and confident in approaching others.

- ♦ You were precocious and carried on long conversations with others.

- ♦ You saw yourself as the "star" and had a flair for the dramatic.

Part 2. These experiences suggest ways in which behavioral patterns develop. Think about how you were treated as a child, your reactions to life, or the things you were rewarded or punished for. What are some habits or behavioral patterns you may have developed? List below some possible habits that you developed as you grew up and how those habits may contribute to your depression. Doing this can hint at the types of responses to life situations that may currently make you feel stuck in the depression loop.

_____

_____

_____

_____

_____

_____

What about Your Thoughts and Your Beliefs?

Another treatment for depression, called "cognitive therapy" (Beck et al. 1979), focuses on changing the way people think about themselves, the world around them, and the future. Cognitive therapy has been well researched and shown to be effective. However, there is no research that shows that changing the way people think is necessary to treat depression. In fact, the research studies that inspired this workbook (Jacobson et al. 1996) show that changing the way people behave is equally effective. In addition, there is good evidence that changing behavior also leads to changes in the way people think, and vice versa. Which approach is most effective for a particular person depends on a number of factors, many of which have yet to be determined by research studies. However, one important issue is how much sense the approach makes to you and whether it fits your understanding of your situation. We encourage you to consider our approach to ending depression by reading the next few chapters and trying the exercises.

Does This Sound Way Too Simple?

Sometimes when we discuss this approach with people, we hear, "It sounds like you're saying that all I have to do is act differently. I've heard things like that before—people telling me I need to pull myself up by my bootstraps, get my act together, look on the bright side, and other stuff like that. If it were that easy, don't they think I would have done it by now? There's got to be more to this than calling some friends, or going to the movies more often."

When people ask us if our approach is simple, we typically say, "Yes and no." It is true that the basic idea is very simple, and very powerful: What you do in your life, and how you do it, makes a difference in how you feel. However, changing your behavior in a meaningful way is not always so simple. It takes patience, awareness, creativity, and a willingness to try new things without any guarantees. Also, it often takes help. When people come to work with us, we assume that they are working hard to overcome their depression. If they're finding it difficult to change, there are good reasons why.

If you've ever tried to quit smoking, or conquer an alcohol or drug problem, or change the way you act in an important relationship, or commit to an exercise or diet program, or develop any other new set of behaviors, you know that change is difficult for many reasons. First, behaviors are like habits. They're often automatic and occur without you being aware of them. Another way of saying this is that your behaviors are part of a well-developed repertoire that has existed for some time. Just as a musician might practice a new piece to make it part of his or her musical repertoire, so you need to practice new behaviors to expand your behavioral repertoire. Second, meaningful change always involves some risk. At the very least, you risk experiencing uncomfortable emotions or situations that you typically are able to avoid.

Third, and perhaps most importantly, it is often not clear what behaviors need to change or how best to go about changing them. What if, for example, a man wanted to spend more time with his family? How should he go about making this change in his life? He would first need to figure out what spending more time with family actually means. Does it mean spending more time doing anything with anyone in the family, or more-specific things with specific family members? Where should he start? What are some reasonable goals to set? How will he know if the change is working? These sorts of issues, and many others, come up whenever you try to change behavior. As strange as it may sound, it makes sense that most people are not that good at changing behavior by themselves. It can be a huge help to have the assistance of an expert, such as a therapist, or the guidance of an established approach like the one described in this workbook.

But Doesn't Depression Cause Behavior, and Not the Other Way Around?

In this culture, there's an assumption that feelings are most often the causes of behavior, rather than the other way around. This idea is taken as so obviously true that people rarely stop to question it. If someone asks why you are scowling (a behavior), you might say it's because you're angry (a feeling). When you cry (a behavior), you probably assume it's because you're sad (a feeling). Similarly, if someone asks why you're staying home rather than going out, you might say it's because you're depressed. What you may not realize is that behavior can just as easily lead to feelings. For example, research has shown that when people are led to smile, without being aware that they're doing so, they report feeling happier (Strack, Martin, and Stepper 1988). Of course, we know that there's much more to ending depression than smiling and acting happy. Still, changing behavior can have a dramatic effect on how you feel, and vice versa. It's not worth getting hung up on which comes first.

OUTSIDE IN VS. INSIDE OUT

The belief that medication is required to treat depression can be referred to as an inside-out approach to change. This view holds that you have to change what is on the inside (your biology) before you can make a behavioral change. The expression "I just don't feel motivated" suggests the same. In Western culture especially, if you don't feel like doing something, you often just refrain from doing it. This idea that how you feel on the inside influences what you do on the outside can start at a very early age. How many times did you hear your mother say, "Do your homework," when your reply was something like "I don't want to do it right now"? Thus, there is an expectation that you need to feel a change in mood, motivation, or drive before making a change in your behavior.

However, as we've stated previously, it is not clear whether brain chemicals cause moods or moods change the levels of brain chemicals. What works from the inside out can also work from the outside in. For example, even if you don't feel motivated to organize files in your home office (an internal feeling), you can nevertheless plan a time to get started on the task of putting hanging files in alphabetical order (an external behavior) and placing financial records, receipts, and so on into files accordingly. Feeling motivated and doing the activity can be completely unrelated to one another. Your brain can interpret the letters on the folders to put them in alphabetical order, your fingers can grasp the papers, you can place papers in files and files in a cabinet drawer, all without feeling at all motivated. This is working from the outside. It may be that as you get closer to completing the job, you will actually feel the motivation that you lacked before beginning. This would be having an effect from the outside in, where doing a behavior changed how you felt inside. Self-activation makes use of this outside-in approach to overcome depression. The assumption is that changes in actions can lead to changes in feelings.

CHAPTER SUMMARY

There are multiple causes for depression. Whatever the cause, depression is a problem between you and your life; it's not a problem inside you. You can overcome depression by recognizing behavioral habits that you have developed over your lifetime and learning to change them. Using guided activity to change behaviors can help you to feel better and improve various life situations that have previously kept you feeling stuck. Guided activity works from the outside in to improve your mood by changing what you do.

Chapter 2

Learn Your Patterns and Start to Change Them

This chapter guides you through the process of learning about your behavioral patterns. The self-activation approach depends on you becoming an expert on how your particular experience of depression works. Before you can make changes to powerfully improve your mood, you have to know what changes to make and how to go about making them. First you need a structured way to track the things you do on a daily basis and how they affect your mood. This will help you to identify situations and behaviors that tend to make you feel more or less depressed. You will then devise a plan to test the effects of making small changes in your activities.

HOW IT WORKS

A client named Ken has suffered intermittently from depression since his early twenties. Now in his middle thirties, Ken lives alone, but has several close friends and generally does well in his life. He has a degree in computer programming, and for several years he was making a good living in that profession. However, during the economic downturn and the fall of the dot-com industry, Ken, like many other Americans, was laid off with little prospect for finding a new job. Ken and David had been workout buddies and met regularly at the gym on weekends. Two weeks into his unemployment, Ken planned to meet David at the gym at their regular time. He arrived fifteen minutes late, which was unusual for him. In fact, he was usually a few minutes early and busily stretching when David went to the locker room to change clothes. This day at the gym Ken was not only late but he had low energy and complained about his former employer, the weather, and the amount of weight he had been gaining. He also complained about the city, his difficulty in finding a date, and how crowded the gym was. David, a psychotherapist, made it a point not to play therapist with his friends, but this situation cried out for the simple question, "Ken, do you think you might be depressed?" Ken answered in the affirmative.

They started their workout, and David changed the conversation to the topic of the various exercises they would do that day. They also began to talk about a movie that David had seen. The conversation interested Ken because he was a fan of the actress starring in the movie. He knew a vast amount of trivia about the actress and told David several behind-the-scenes stories about the actress. After about thirty minutes into the workout, Ken's mood began to shift. He started to talk about plans for seeing upcoming movies, and he asked David if he was interested in going for a short walk at the lake following the workout. Then they had a discussion about how the combination of physical exercise (which dealt directly with Ken's weight gain) and socializing (which dealt with his feelings of isolation) made him feel much better than staying at home or complaining. Ken said that he felt considerably better after the workout activity than he had when he had begun.

Behavioral Patterns

Ken's story is not unusual. When he was feeling depressed, Ken tended to engage in activities such as worrying, expressing negative feelings about situations, or simply sitting and staring out the window. But if someone asked him how he spent his time with David, Ken would probably say he was "working out." The problem here is that working out was only part of the story. What Ken also did with David was behave in many of the same ways he behaved elsewhere—complaining, worrying, looking downward with his eyes—the very behaviors that put Ken at risk for depression and would help keep him stuck in it once it started. Ken didn't behave this way because he was a weak or whiny person. Ken's depressed behavior was, in many ways, no different from any other behavior, depressive or not. Ken was responding to his environment, and to his feelings. When he felt down, he acted accordingly. Engaging with David at the gym improved his mood. He didn't need to understand where the feelings came from, but he needed to understand what he could do about them. In the future, it would be important for Ken to recognize when he was shutting down and acting in a way that made him feel more depressed, so he could change those behaviors. Without David around to tell him he seemed depressed, Ken would need to recognize the signs on his own.

Three Important Principles of Behavior

Ken's story illustrates three important behavioral principles:

1. Much of your behavior is so automatic that it occurs outside of your awareness.

2. You do much of what you do out of habit.

3. To change behavioral habits, you must first recognize the behavorial pattern, so you can know when and what to change.

Just because depressed behavior looks different from "happy" behavior doesn't mean the two operate differently. Many of the things that people do when they aren't depressed also happen outside of their awareness and can be understood as habits. Therefore, these three principles of behavior can be applied to the experience and treatment of depression.

STEPS TO INCREASING YOUR BEHAVIORAL AWARENESS

It may sound odd to say that people act without being aware of the acting, or that you must increase your awareness. Consider, however, the act of driving your car. When you first learned how to drive your car, you needed to read the instructions in a driver's education course, listen to the teacher, perhaps even watch a few graphic videos about traffic accidents. When you took your first practice drive, perhaps with a parent or older sibling or relative, you talked yourself through each step: "Turn on the ignition. Look in the rearview mirror, and turn your head to the right to check behind, to make sure no traffic is coming. Put the gearshift in reverse. Now slowly depress the gas pedal and begin to back out," and so on. You had to think about what to do before turning right or left, coming to a stop or yield sign, allowing another driver to pass, and all of the multiple and complex details involved in driving a car safely.

Once you mastered driving the car, however, the activity became more automatic. In fact, the only time that an experienced driver is likely to have to talk himself or herself through the steps of driving is when there has been a major shift in the context of the situation. For example, if there is a blizzard, an experienced driver may consciously think to "turn into the skid" if the car begins to slide. Apart from unfamiliar situations, however, the behavior of driving a car is done with very little thought.

Most of the behaviors that you engage in during the day are habits that you do automatically. You probably go directly to the cupboard where you keep your coffee cup or cereal each morning, and you get the milk out of the refrigerator without thinking about it. Your soap, deodorant, and toothbrush are most likely in the same place, and you simply reach for them without having to direct yourself through the steps. You might be amazed at how much of life you live on automatic pilot.

Checkpoint

Does the goal of increasing awareness of your behavior patterns seem valuable to you?

Yes _____ No _____

As with so many other actions, habits that keep you depressed are also practiced without your awareness. This book will help you recognize your depressed habits and replace them with healthier habits that can lead to greater contentment or happiness.

Step 1: Track Your Activities on a Day-to-Day, Hour-by-Hour Basis

It helps to track the behaviors you engage in each day. To do this, you can use an activity monitoring chart (Beck et al. 1979). Later in this chapter, you will find a blank chart to copy and use to record your activities. For now, take a look at the activity monitoring chart below. This chart was completed by a client named Lisa as part of her self-activation work. We have included her notes for Sunday. Notice that she has completed a word or two about each hour of the day. She wrote down what she was doing, where she was, and who she was with. The chart is detailed but not overly so. There is enough information to track her day, and for her to begin to see what she has done and how it may effect her mood.

Lisa's Activity Monitoring Chart

Time	Sunday
Midnight	In bed alone
1:00 A.M.	Asleep
2:00 A.M.	Asleep
3:00 A.M.	Asleep
4:00 A.M.	Asleep
5:00 A.M.	Awake, lying in bed, staring into space
6:00 A.M.	Up to get water in kitchen
7:00 A.M.	Dozing in bed
8:00 A.M.	Up, drinking coffee in kitchen
9:00 A.M.	Back to bed
10:00 A.M.	On the phone with Ellen
11:00 A.M.	Going to Ellen's
Noon	With Ellen at brunch at café
1:00 P.M.	To laundromat, then home

2:00 P.M.	Home alone
3:00 P.M.	Back to laundromat, alone
4:00 P.M.	Nap
5:00 P.M.	Watching TV in bedroom
6:00 P.M.	TV, bored
7:00 P.M.	TV
8:00 P.M.	Read, fall asleep
9:00 P.M.	TV
10:00 P.M.	Take a bath
11:00 P.M.	Go to bed

To complete an activity monitoring chart, you simply enter the particular behaviors or activities that you engaged in for each hour of the day. The more detail you add, the better, but don't feel that you have to document everything perfectly. When you're depressed, the last thing you need is one more performance expectation or added stress. What you do need are some successes in changing the way you feel, and this is the first step toward that goal. You need to become aware of what you're doing in a deeper way than you have up until now. For example, what's the first thing that comes into your mind if someone were to ask you, "What did you do yesterday afternoon?"

If you said something like, "I worked," or "I stayed at home," or "I slept," then your challenge is to get more specific in your awareness of your own activities. For example, what exactly did you do at work or at home at different points during the day? When were you alone and when were you with other people? Rather than saying, "I stayed at home," you may realize that you lay down on the couch for thirty minutes, then watched television for an hour, then spoke to a friend on the phone for a few minutes, then cleaned up the garage, and so on. Why do such things matter? Because they are the fabric through which depression habits are woven. To unravel them, you must understand how they all tie together.

Exercise: Monitoring Your Activity: Getting the Details

Look back closely at the last twenty-four hours of your life and complete the activity monitoring chart below. Make sure to write down what you were doing and with whom, if anyone, you were doing it. For now, you might just make a mental note of how each activity felt. For example, how depressed did you feel during each activity? What other sorts of emotions arose? Write down everything you did yesterday in the column on the left marked "yesterday." Ignore the right-hand column for now.

Activity Monitoring Chart

Time	Yesterday	Today
Midnight		
1:00 A.M.		
2:00 A.M.		
3:00 A.M.		
4:00 A.M.		
5:00 A.M.		
6:00 A.M.		
7:00 A.M.		
8:00 A.M.		
9:00 A.M.		
10:00 A.M.		
11:00 A.M.		
Noon		
1:00 P.M.		
2:00 P.M.		
3:00 P.M.		
4:00 P.M.		
5:00 P.M.		
6:00 P.M.		
7:00 P.M.		
8:00 P.M.		
9:00 P.M.		
10:00 P.M.		
11:00 P.M.		

Take a look at what you've written down. How detailed is it? What do you notice? Often, people will notice that they have engaged in many more or many fewer activities than they would have thought possible. For example, the first time our client, Mark, monitored his behavior over the last twenty-four hours, he noticed that he had engaged in a wide range of activities at work and at home. He never stuck to one thing for more than thirty minutes. In addition, Mark was alone the overwhelming majority of the time. The same pattern emerged when he tracked an entire week of his behavior.

Another client, Lucia, saw that she had actually engaged in a much smaller range of activities than she had assumed. In fact, she had spent the bulk of her waking hours on both days sitting alone on her couch watching television and eating. As her self-awareness increased, Lucia realized that watching television was an ingrained habit that helped her to avoid dealing with other issues that caused her anxiety or made her feel sad. When Lucia began to slowly break down the pattern and substitute new ways of coping, her mood improved a great deal. Instead of watching television and eating in the early evening, she began taking a short walk around the block before dark. She also started writing short stories as an alternative to watching television. She discovered that making up characters gave her something to look forward to each evening as her plots developed in the stories she was writing.

Checkpoint

Have you ever noticed how changing what you're doing or where you're doing it can have a positive effect on your mood, even if it's a small one?

Yes _____   No _____

Exercise: Monitoring Your Activity in Even Greater Detail

Let's look at the difference in amount of detail you can remember from day to day. Go back to the activity monitoring chart in the last exercise. You have completed the chart for everything that you did yesterday. Perhaps you learned that it is harder to remember details than you would think. Now think back over the previous three or four hours. What have you been doing during this time? Try to recall as many details as you can about what you did, where you did it, and with whom. Write this down next to the corresponding hour in the column marked "Today." When you have completed this exercise, think about whether it was easier for you to recall details from yesterday or from the previous three or four hours. Which information do you believe is more accurate? You might notice that it was easier to note activities in greater detail when you only thought about the previous few hours than when you tried to remember what happened on a previous day. The point is that it is good to recognize behavior as it occurs or soon thereafter. Although it may be unrealistic to carry an activity chart with you wherever you go, the sooner you can make a few notes on your chart, the better.

Step 2: Become Aware of Behavior-Mood Links

By now you should be familiar with the idea that what you do affects how you feel. For example, it's very hard to feel relaxed if you furrow your brow and tighten your shoulders. It's easier to feel relaxed if you loosen your muscles and focus on pleasant images. Similarly, it's hard (though not impossible) to feel depressed if you are actively engaged in something pleasurable. We recognize that many activities that provide pleasure when you are not depressed may not be pleasurable when you are feeling depressed. As you work through this program and begin to reengage, you may start to participate in activities that once brought pleasure. Whether you feel pleasure or a sense of accomplishment from the activity will depend on how consistently you practice activating, regardless of how it immediately makes you feel. For now, just note that it's easier to feel depressed if you sit by yourself worrying about being depressed.

You should also know by now that we don't think behavior change is easy. Ending depression is more than just acting happy. Nonetheless, increasing your awareness of the effect of your current behavior on your mood can help you recognize when certain behaviors are betraying you rather than helping. Remember Ken's situation from the beginning of this chapter? When Ken met David at the gym, he was engaging in a social interaction and physical activity. The conversation made him feel engaged, and the workout gave him energy. Ken's conversation with David also provided him with a new plan to recognize when he was shutting down, and he made a commitment to himself to try to engage in an activity that might make him feel better. He saw that how he acted affected how he felt, and he was determined to change what he could, even though his current unemployment was stressful and discouraging.

An activity monitoring chart can be a very useful way to begin to understand your mood-behavior links. In fact, it is more accurate to call it an activity-*and-mood* monitoring chart. Take a look at the example below completed by Nathan. Nathan was forty-one years old and recently divorced. He worked as an advertising salesperson. Although Nathan worked for a firm, most of his job was focused on his own sales, and he worked almost entirely on commission. When Nathan first began his work on self-activation, he described himself as "always depressed. I can't ever seem to snap out of it. No matter where I am, it always seems to find me." For each weekday, Nathan recorded the activities he engaged in and the feelings or emotions he experienced while engaging in the activities. He rated the intensity of each feeling on a scale of 1 to 10, with 1 being the least intense he ever felt the emotion and 10 being the most intense. Nathan completed the activity chart periodically on Sunday through Wednesday.

Nathan's Activity-and-Mood Monitoring Chart

Hours	Sunday	Monday	Tuesday	Wednesday
7:00 A.M. **Activity**	Ate breakfast—toast Read newspaper in kitchen	Ate breakfast— muffin Read newspaper in kitchen	Ate breakfast—cold cereal Read newspaper in kitchen	Ate breakfast—toast Read newspaper in kitchen
Mood	Depressed 6	Depressed 6	Depressed 6	Depressed 6
8:00 A.M. **Activity**	Dressing in bedroom Driving to work, expressway	Dressing in bedroom Driving to work, expressway	Dressing in bedroom Driving to work, expressway	Dressing in bedroom Driving to work, expressway
Mood	Depressed 8	Depressed 8	Depressed 8	Depressed 8
9:00 A.M. **Activity**	Coffee at snack bar	Meetings at office until noon	Coffee at latte stand, sat at table outside	On the road all day, expressway and a few major city streets
Mood	Relaxed 5 Depressed 1	Depressed 5	Mellow 6	Depressed 3
10:00 A.M. **Activity**	Worked on report	Meetings	Meeting with boss in boardroom	On the road
Mood	Depressed 5	Depressed 5	Depressed 8	Depressed 3
11:00 A.M. **Activity**			Sat at desk, not getting work done	On the road
Mood			Depressed 8	Depressed 3 Interested 5
Noon **Activity**			Went home sick	On the road, ran a few personal errands at lunchtime
Mood			Depressed 9	Depressed 2 Accomplished 3
1:00 P.M. **Activity**			Slept until 5:30	
Mood				

6:00 P.M. Activity	Ate dinner at kitchen table—piece of salmon and broccoli	Ate dinner at kitchen table— grilled chicken and a potato	Ate dinner—frozen pot pie Drank a beer Sitting on sofa with local news on television	Ate dinner at kitchen table— chicken breast and carrots, dinner salad
Mood	Depressed 7	Depressed 6	Depressed 10	Depressed 3
7:00 P.M. Activity	Watched TV until bedtime—some reality show	Watched TV until bedtime—reruns of 1970s sitcoms		Saw movie with friend Dana—action/ adventure flick
Mood	Depressed 7	Depressed 8		Depressed 1 Happy 4

What do you notice about the links between Nathan's behavior and his mood? We noticed several things. First, Nathan generally woke up depressed and went to bed depressed. This pattern clearly needed to be changed because mornings and evenings were his only times away from work. Moreover, the pattern probably contributed to Nathan's sense that he was "always depressed." The second thing we noticed was that there was actually quite a bit of variation in how depressed he felt during the week. For example, on Wednesday, once Nathan started working around nine o'clock, his depression level dropped to a 3 and remained that way or lower throughout the rest of the day, compared to the 5 to 8 levels on other days. This also happened to be the only day he was working outside the office and meeting many different clients on the road.

A small yet important difference occurred on those days that Nathan began his workday with a cup of coffee. When Nathan got coffee, he noticed feeling relaxed or mellow and the depression lifted somewhat, albeit briefly. Nathan became aware that part of what he liked about those few minutes was the opportunity to socialize with his coworkers, something he didn't have much time to do given the amount of time he spent working on sales by himself. While drinking coffee, Nathan and his coworkers often shared some of the common work stresses they were going through. Nathan experienced these conversations as support and validation.

Finally, how Nathan responded to feeling depressed seemed to have an effect on how he would feel in the near future. For example, on Tuesday, Nathan had a particularly difficult meeting with his boss, during which he was told that he needed to increase his productivity by completing more sales. For the hour directly after the meeting, Nathan sat at his desk doing nothing except reliving the conversation with his boss in his head and worrying about his future. His depression stayed steady at an 8 out of 10. Then Nathan went home sick for the day (depression level 9) and slept the rest of the afternoon. When he woke up, he ate dinner and drank beer (depression level 10).

What would have happened if, rather than sitting at his desk replaying events mentally, worrying, going home, sleeping, and drinking beer, Nathan immediately began to make more calls or invited a friend out to lunch, or did some other activity designed to get him reengaged in his life? Perhaps it wouldn't have made any difference in his mood. Perhaps it would have helped him feel slightly less depressed, which could have, in turn, helped him have the energy to stay at work and complete some tasks, which would help him feel productive. It was impossible to know without doing some experimenting. But at the time, it was very clear that Nathan had experienced a sort of mini–depression loop. His attempts to cope with depression that day seemed to make him feel worse. In contrast, during dinner on Wednesday evening, Nathan's depression level was a 3. Rather than watching television (his usual pattern), Nathan decided to call a friend and see a movie. During his time out with his friend, Nathan reported that he felt happy for the first time all week and his depression level dropped to a 1.

Exercise: Monitoring Your Activity and Mood during the Week

Over the next week, complete the activity-and-mood monitoring chart below at least three times a day (some people find it helpful to complete the chart at lunchtime, dinnertime, and just before going to bed). The more often you can enter information in the chart, the better, because trying to remember exactly what you did several hours ago and how you felt can be quite difficult when you're depressed. Record each activity in a single box. If you engaged in an activity for more than one hour, leave the next hour blank or draw a line through it indicating that the previous behavior continued. You should still record your mood, however. If you do several different things in an hour, write down as many as you can (particularly if you felt differently during different activities).

For each activity, write down a word or two to describe how you felt, and rate the intensity of the feeling on a scale of 1 to 10, with 1 being the least intense you've ever felt it and 10 being the most intense. To help with this, here is a list of common feeling words:

sadness	glad	anger	anxious
embarrassed	pleased	rageful	fearful
shamed	happy	furious	scared
despairing	joyful	cross	terrified
melancholy	elated	vexed	nervous
blue	excited	incensed	apprehensive
gloomy	passionate	irate	alarmed

In order to provide ample space for writing, the activity-and-mood monitoring chart allows for only one day. Please make multiple copies of this form before writing on the chart.

We recommend that you read no further in this workbook until you have completed at least a week of activity and mood monitoring. The strategies that follow depend on you having a greater awareness of your behavior-mood links. The next week might also be a good time to review the information we've covered up until this point. Copies of monitoring forms are provided in the appendix for photocopying.

Activity-and-Mood Monitoring Chart

Before writing on the activity-and-mood monitoring chart, you should make photocopies so that you can use it again. You will use this chart in later exercises. In each box write the activities you engaged in during the hour, and how you felt. Rate your feeling on a scale of 1 to 10, with 1 being the least intensity of feeling and 10 being the most.

Time	Day and Date:
Midnight	
Mood	
1:00 A.M.	
Mood	
2:00 A.M.	
Mood	
3:00 A.M.	
Mood	
4:00 A.M.	
Mood	
5:00 A.M.	
Mood	
6:00 A.M.	
Mood	
7:00 A.M.	
Mood	
8:00 A.M.	
Mood	
9:00 A.M.	
Mood	
10:00 A.M.	
Mood	

11:00 A.M.	
Mood	
Noon	
Mood	
1:00 P.M.	
Mood	
2:00 P.M.	
Mood	
3:00 P.M.	
Mood	
4:00 P.M.	
Mood	
5:00 P.M.	
Mood	
6:00 P.M.	
Mood	
7:00 P.M.	
Mood	
8:00 P.M.	
Mood	
9:00 P.M.	
Mood	
10:00 P.M.	
Mood	
11:00 P.M.	
Mood	

Different Feelings Can Occur with Different Activities

People experience emotions with varying intensity based upon the situations in which they occur. For example, you might be out on a sunny summer day and eat a piece of your favorite, juicy, summer fruit. The feelings associated with it may be satisfaction and pleasure. On such a day, you might rate both feelings as 10 on the 1 to 10 scale. However, if you are rushing through a busy workday, feeling pressured to get things accomplished, and you pick up a piece of the same kind of fruit at your local deli, you may still experience satisfaction and pleasure but might rate both only a 2 or 3 in intensity. So, when you try to rate the intensity of your emotions on your activity-and-mood monitoring charts, remember to consider the entire context of the situation and then rate the intensity of what you are feeling.

Checkpoint

Have you learned anything new about links between your activities and your moods?

Yes _____ No _____

What Did You Notice?

Increasing awareness of behavior-mood links for the first time can be a real eye-opener. Some of the most common things people notice are listed below:

- variations in mood

- lack of variations in mood

- difficult times of day

- easier times of day

- difficult situations or activities

- enjoyable situations or activities

- depression loops

You may have noticed much more variation in your mood than you would have predicted. Depression has a way of coloring memory as you look back in time, even over a few hours. Like Nathan, you may have the sense that you are "always depressed." However, when you record your experiences close to the time that they happen, you may find your mood is much more variable. Even if your mood is generally depressed (as opposed to happy, relaxed, angry, or otherwise), the *level* of depression will probably vary, even if it's only slightly. These variations are important because they provide clues about situations, activities, or times of day that can increase or decrease your depression. Those situations, activities, or times that increase depression can be modified, and those that decrease it can be capitalized on in ways we will discuss shortly.

Sometimes people notice that there is a real lack of variation in the way they feel. For example, one man with whom we worked recorded feeling only depressed or bored all the time. Although the level of boredom or depression varied somewhat, the range of emotional experiences did not. Part of his self-activation strategy, therefore, involved finding activities and situations that produced other sorts of emotional experiences. For example, as an experiment, he purposely went to a comedy club with friends to see if humor had an effect on the range of his moods.

You probably noticed difficult times of day on your activity-and-mood monitoring chart. You may find that you associate morning with feelings of depression. Or you may associate depression with returning home at the end of the day or eating dinner. Other times of day may be somewhat better. One of our clients, Dana, found that her mood was significantly less depressed for a brief period of time each day when she was at the gym. After examining her experiences at the gym a little more closely, Dana became aware that while she was working out she wasn't thinking about the things that tended to depress her. She was then able to introduce other sorts of enjoyable activities that occupied her mind at other points in her week.

More on the Depression Loop

One of the most important things to become aware of as you monitor your activities is the presence of depression loops. Again, depression loops occur when attempts to cope with difficult or painful feelings actually make depression worse. This happens because the attempts to cope, although they may temporarily help you escape from emotional pain or discomfort, actually make things worse in the long run. They either don't solve a problem that needs solving, or they create additional problems that leave you at risk for depression.

As you look back over your activity-and-mood monitoring chart, look for times when you felt more than a little depressed. Then look at what you did immediately following those times. Did your mood improve, stay the same, or get worse over the next hour or two? How about over the course of the day? If your mood got better, it's probably because either the situation changed, or the way you responded to things made a difference. If your mood got worse, did it have something to do with how you responded to depressed feelings or a difficult situation? For example, many people cope with a depressed mood by withdrawing or otherwise trying to escape from feelings or situations. These escape behaviors could include sleeping, removing yourself from social situations, using alcohol or drugs, or any other behavior that temporarily removes you from what you want to avoid. If you notice any behaviors such as these or others that help you escape but make depression worse, don't be ashamed or self-critical. Escape and avoidance behaviors are natural responses to depression. And they work in the short run. We'll have much more to say about escape and avoidance in chapter 3.

BEGIN TO EXPERIMENT: MAKING STRATEGIC CHANGES

If what you do affects how you feel, then changing what you're doing (or how you're doing it) can have an effect on your mood. The remainder of this book is about doing precisely this: making strategic changes in the way you behave on a day-to-day basis. It is best to begin with experimenting and keeping your goals modest. For now, the goal is not to completely overcome your depression. Instead, you should be looking for small manageable changes you can try out to see if they have even a small positive effect on your mood. Your goal is to find ways to begin to unravel your depression. If you follow the seven steps below it will be easier to make the changes you need to make.

Step 1: Identify Situations and Behaviors That Depress You

There are situations in life, such as living in chronic poverty or having a home destroyed by a natural disaster, that would be upsetting to anyone. Often it is what you do in a distressing situation that may make you more or less depressed. For example, someone living in poverty who saves as much money as possible on simple meals, tries to keep a very small room in a boarding house clean and neat, or spends time telling stories to children may feel a little better about his or her situation than someone who drinks and sleeps at various tolerant but mostly unkind relatives' homes.

Exercise: Finding the Behaviors That Make You Feel Bad

Look back over the activity-and-mood monitoring charts you completed over the last week. Choose one or two situations and corresponding behaviors that seemed to make your mood worse. If your mood was steadily depressed with little variation, pick a situation and behavior that clearly did nothing to improve your mood and could be changed. Try to find behaviors that occur somewhat regularly during your week. You're looking for regular patterns that can be changed. In the spaces below, fill in the days of the week and time of day, the situations in which the behaviors occur, and your current behaviors in the situations. For now, leave blank the space for alternative behaviors. As with the activity-and-mood monitoring chart, try to be as detailed as possible.

Day(s) of week and time of day: _____

Situation: _____

Current behavior: _____

Alternative behaviors: _____

_____

_____

_____

Day(s) of week and time of day: _____

Situation: _____

Current behavior: _____

Alternative behaviors: _____

_____

_____

_____

Step 2: Alternative Behaviors

For every behavior that makes you feel badly, there is some alternative behavior that can either make you feel better or improve your life situation. If your kitchen is a mess and there are dirty dishes piled in the sink, turning away from it all and taking a nap is likely to make you feel more depressed in the long run. However, if you simply wash and dry the glassware, or the silverware, even if you leave the other dishes unattended to, it may bring a sense of relief or at least make an improvement in the state of your kitchen.

Exercise: Finding Alternative Behaviors

For each situation and behavior, think of as many alternative behaviors as you can and write them down in the space that you left blank in the previous exercise. Try not to judge whether particular behaviors will be helpful. At this point, you want to brainstorm and include as many alternatives as possible. Try to think of behaviors that may help to improve your mood, but include behaviors that may worsen your mood or have no effect at all. The goal is to be as open-minded as possible about alternatives.

Lisa's Example

Below is an example of how Lisa completed the previous exercises.

Day(s) of week and time of day: *Monday–Friday 6:00–7:00 P.M.*

Situation: *At home after work*

Current behavior: *Watch TV*

Alternative behaviors: *Lie in bed, go jogging, pay bills, walk to the coffee shop, call friends/family, catch up on work, clean the house, work in the garden*

Day(s) of week and time of day: *Saturday/Sunday 7:00–9:00 A.M.*

Situation: *At home on the weekend mornings*

Current behavior: *Lie in bed, drink coffee*

Alternative behaviors: *Take dog to the park, make breakfast and read the paper, go jogging, watch television, clean the house*

When Lisa started to think of alternative behaviors for each situation, she began to feel some relief and a small amount of hopefulness even though she hadn't made any changes yet. When people are depressed, they often feel that they don't have any choices and that they cannot take control of their lives to make even the smallest changes. Alternatively, because they are depressed, they doubt that they will ever feel motivated enough to follow through with any changes, or they have very little confidence that anything will make a difference. As a result, they may not even take the time to think about possible changes they could make. When Lisa started listing options, including behaviors that could potentially make her more depressed, she sensed a little more control over her mood. She realized that she had options and that the choice of how to behave was hers.

Step 3: Select Alternative Behaviors and Schedule Them into Your Week

Look over your list of alternative behaviors for each situation. Which behaviors might have the potential to improve your mood, even slightly? Which ones might leave you as depressed as or even more depressed than you typically are in each situation? For each situation, choose an alternative behavior that might have a positive effect on your mood. Make sure that the behavior is relatively easy to do. For example, deciding to work out five days a week for an hour a day may be too difficult a change to make if you are currently doing no exercise. Only choose alternative behaviors that you are reasonably sure you can do. What you need now are successes, however small, rather than lofty goals that you will have difficulty reaching. Once you have a few successes under your belt and are feeling more in control of your mood, you can move on to bigger challenges.

When Lisa looked at her list of alternative behaviors several things occurred to her. First, when it came to the weekday evenings from six to seven, she realized that lying in bed, paying bills, or catching up on work wasn't going to help her mood. She worked hard all day and wanted to do something enjoyable during this time. She also realized that jogging could improve her mood, but it might also make her more depressed because she felt so out of shape. She decided to try walking to the coffee shop or calling friends or family for the first two nights of the week, and jogging on the third night. Lisa scheduled these activities into an activity monitoring chart for the coming week. She then made a written contract with herself that looked like this:

As an experiment, I will either walk to the coffee shop or phone my friends or family on Monday and Tuesday from 6:00 to 7:00 P.M. On Wednesday night, I will jog during this time. My goal is to see how these activities affect my mood.

—Lisa Smith

Lisa made a similar plan for Saturday and Sunday morning. She scheduled the alternative activities into her calendar and made a written contract with herself. The idea of making a contract with yourself may seem a little odd. However, research has shown that making behavioral-change commitments more formal increases the likelihood that you will carry them through (Schlenker, Dlugolecki, and Doherty 1994). Stating them publicly increases the odds even further. Thus, Lisa made a contract not because she doubted her ability to make changes or because she was so weak willed that she couldn't follow through without one. She wrote a contract because it was a way to help her follow through on her experiment. Lisa was doing herself a favor.

Step 4: Adopt an Experimental Attitude

It is crucial that you adopt an experimental attitude. To do so means becoming interested in the outcome no matter what the results are. In other words, whether the alternative behavior has a positive effect on your mood or not, you know you have learned something important. The experiment is not a test of your willpower or a test of whether self-activation is the right approach for you. It is simply a way of seeing whether or not particular behaviors affect your mood. The results can then be used to try other experiments and to include specific changes in your strategy for ending depression.

Sometimes when you are depressed the strength of certain emotions can make it difficult to adopt an experimental attitude. The power of hopeless thoughts and feelings can make changes seem doomed to failure ("I know this won't work, so why try?"). Depression may have a way of making everything seem like a test of your worthiness ("The fact that this didn't work just shows how weak willed I am").

When you're depressed, your feelings often aren't a good basis for judging how helpful changes can be. Depression can be a lot like that little devil on your shoulder trying to convince you that nothing will work, things can't improve, and it's all your fault. If this happens to you, we suggest that you spend no energy trying to argue with the devil on your shoulder. Trying to convince yourself that things will work, or that it's not your fault, or that you really should have a more positive attitude just keeps the argument going. Instead, just let the little devil have his say while you continue to plan for and begin the experiment. If you don't involve yourself in the argument by trying to win it, the negative messages will eventually drift away. Another useful thing to do is to commit yourself to changes, regardless of how you feel. We'll have much more to say about this later. For now, the main idea is that acting on your plan can potentially have a positive effect on your mood.

Finally, adopting an experimental attitude also means keeping your expectations modest. Don't expect the changes you make to turn you into a happy-go-lucky person overnight. Again, the goal is to see what sorts of small changes can affect your mood in particular situations. Even though this is a relatively small step in the path to ending depression, it is a critical one.

Step 5: Try Out the New Behaviors and Observe Their Effects

Once you have made a commitment to conduct an experiment, it is time to try the new behaviors and observe their effects.

Exercise: Planning for the Week

You can now use some blank activity-and-mood monitoring charts to plan some activities and make commitments to when you will do them. You can use the chart like a planner or scheduler. Write down the changes you plan to make in the coming week on the particular days and times that you plan to do them (you will need enough charts to schedule activities for each day). As you do the new activities, be sure to monitor your moods. Continue to monitor your activities and moods for those times when you do not plan an activity.

You may notice a positive effect from some of these new activities. Some activities can give you a sense of accomplishment. Getting dirty dishes cleaned and put in cabinets may make you feel like you've accomplished something even in the midst of depression. Other activities, such as listening to a piece of music that you enjoy, may bring you pleasure. Activities can result in feelings of both accomplishment and pleasure, such as working out did for Ken. He took pleasure in the activity and also felt that he had accomplished progress toward his overall physical fitness.

There are three very important things you need to do when changing your behavior. The first is to become as fully involved as possible in the new activity when you're doing it. Focus on what you're doing rather than on things that happened in the past or might happen in the future. For example, if you spend all your time during a walk thinking about things that make you depressed, you aren't really taking a walk. You just happen to be walking while your real focus is on what's going through your head. To be involved in a walk means to observe and experience the process of walking itself: seeing what's around you, feeling the wind, sun, or rain, and hearing the sounds of birds or other things in your environment.

The second important thing to do when changing behavior is to avoid evaluating the outcome of the experiment while it's going on. While speaking to friends on the phone (a new behavior), you may find yourself thinking, for example, "This isn't working, because I still feel depressed." When you focus your attention on whether the experiment is "working," you are not involved in what you're doing; you're evaluating it. Instead, allow yourself to experience whatever you experience during a new activity and evaluate it afterwards. How did it feel? What was your mood like during the activity? Did your mood change at any point during the experience? What was your mood like compared to how it usually is during this time of day or in this situation?

The third important thing is to try an experiment more than once. Good scientists always run an experiment more than once, because results can vary. We recommend that you try any new behavior at least three times before drawing any conclusions about how it affects your mood.

Step 6: Evaluate the Results of the Experiment

What did you notice when you tried out the new behaviors? As you experiment with new behaviors, you will continually keep track of the results.

Exercise: Comparing the Results

Rate your mood on the activity-and-mood monitoring chart as soon as possible after completing each of the new behaviors. When you have tried each behavior at least three different times, compare your mood ratings for these times of day or situations with your mood ratings for the same times of day or situations a week ago. What have you learned? Did the experiments have any effect on your mood? If so, did your mood improve or worsen during the experiments?

Step 7: Continue Trying New Experiments

You need to continue experimenting, observing the results, and using results from previous experiments as a point of comparison. This step is an important one. Don't expect a quick fix. Changing the way you respond to events in your life or how you approach things day to day requires practice and experimentation. If the behavioral changes you made initially had a positive effect, you will probably want to continue including them on a regular basis. If they didn't have a positive effect, why not? Below are several reasons why changes you make might not have a positive effect on your mood.

- The new behavior isn't a helpful one.
  Solution: Determine why the behavior wasn't helpful. Think of alternatives and try them out in new experiments.

- You were distracted during the experiment.
  Solution: Practice becoming fully involved in what you're doing. Observe when you are not fully involved and gently focus your attention on what you're doing.

- Your current mood is making it difficult to remember how you felt during the experiment.
  Solution: Ask yourself if your current depressed mood is making it difficult to remember how you felt during the experiment. Imagine the experiment in as much detail as possible, and try to remember how you felt at the time, rather than how you feel about it right now.

We suggest that you continue experimenting for at least two to three weeks. Those changes that improve your mood, even slightly, should be worked into a regular routine.

CHAPTER SUMMARY

What you do on a day-to-day basis has a powerful effect on how you feel. Much of your behavior, including behavior that keeps depression going, is so automatic that you're probably hardly aware of it. Depressed behavior can easily become a habit. The first step to ending depression is increasing your awareness of links between situations, behaviors, and moods. Completing an activity-and-mood monitoring chart several times a day can help you gather reliable information about your depression. Looking closely at the information you gather can reveal patterns that have negative effects on your mood.

Adopting an experimental attitude helps you to try new behaviors and observe their effects without having unrealistic expectations. Whenever you make changes in your activities, you can learn something about how your depression works. By repeating experiments or new behaviors over several days, you can gather reliable information about activities that may have a positive effect on your mood. Once you begin to see that what you do can have a positive effect on how you feel, you will have greater confidence that you can take the next steps toward ending depression.

Part 2

Ending Depression

Chapter 3

Getting Out of "TRAPs" and Back on "TRAC"

Many tasks in life can be tedious or overwhelming. When you're depressed, however, it can feel as if the most basic task is nearly impossible. This chapter looks at avoidance as a psychological or behavioral process at the heart of depression. The goal is to help you to recognize your own avoidance behaviors and give you a simple technique for changing them.

AVOIDANCE IS A POWERFUL HABIT

Leslie was a thirty-three-year-old mother of two. Her eldest child had just entered the second grade and her youngest was in kindergarten. Leslie's husband had a flexible work schedule, mostly working from home over the Internet. Years earlier, following the birth of her second child, Leslie had begun to experience symptoms of depression. She was diagnosed with postpartum depression at that time, and it was believed that her depression would improve with time and medication. It did, somewhat. She was able to take care of her children and even began meeting other mothers for strolls in the park with the baby and with her older child, who was three. But then, a number of major life events slowly brought her down again.

When the baby was six months old, Leslie returned to work part-time. Her new employer allowed her to take extra time from work to take the children to see their doctor, but he was resentful about it. He implied that she was not able to do her job competently and would make statements like, "You only work twenty hours a week. Can't you make appointments during your scheduled time off?" She did, except that sometimes there were emergencies when she needed to take the baby right away. She started arriving at work late because she dreaded the job. Her husband would fix breakfast for their three-year-old while Leslie would remain in bed, waking up just enough to nurse the baby. Her husband did not want to push too hard, but he gently encouraged Leslie to get ready for work. She washed, dressed, and left the house later and later each day. Heavy traffic slowed her down, and she used the traffic as an excuse for her lateness. Her boss was increasingly annoyed with her. After a month of late days, he gave her a verbal warning.

The verbal warning resulted in Leslie dreading work even more. She thought that her boss disliked her, so instead of going to work and making sure that she got the job done properly, she began calling in sick. By the end of a year, Leslie had been written up twice for frequent absences. When she didn't call in at all on one occasion, because her husband had an early meeting away from home and didn't wake her up, Leslie was fired.

After a half-hearted attempt to find a new job, Leslie and her husband decided that she would be happier working at home with the children. However, when her mother died suddenly of a cerebral hemorrhage, Leslie became even more disheartened. Now that the children were both in school at least part of the day, she got less and less accomplished around the house. Her husband took their youngest to and from kindergarten. Their second grader rode the school bus. Leslie awakened each day with the intention of accomplishing a number of chores around the house. However, when it came to cleaning the dishes, she would start and then realize that she needed to do laundry. She'd go to the laundry room, look at the enormous pile of clothes that had gathered, and feel overwhelmed. Not knowing where to place yet another pile of clothes, she'd take a load out of the dryer and notice that they were wrinkled from sitting too long. Folding the clothes didn't help much, but she'd fold half of the load and decide to iron. By this time, Leslie felt overwhelmed and exhausted. She told herself, "I'll just lie down and close my eyes for a few minutes." She would awaken only when her husband came home. In the evening, she spent hours knitting sweaters for the children. She had always enjoyed knitting, and found that this gave her a sense of relaxation and accomplishment in the midst of chaos.

At this point, Leslie's husband was losing patience, and he and Leslie began quarreling. More and more Leslie considered herself a failure at work, as a mother, and as a homemaker. She started staying in bed most of the day. Leslie and her husband became more estranged. He threatened to leave her unless she got help. At his insistence, Leslie entered therapy for her depression.

Looking at the Patterns

Leslie clearly avoided going to work as her discomfort with her boss increased. She also avoided housework because it seemed overwhelming to her. Avoidance behavior is not always this easy to see. The behaviors you engage in will often seem adaptive if you pay attention only to the *appearance* of what you are doing (how can knitting sweaters be avoidance?). However, you may pay less attention to the situations or contexts in which these behaviors are occurring.

For example, what else could you be doing that you might be avoiding? What do you need to do to affect your mood positively or to build the kind of life you want to live? Change is difficult and often creates anxiety. Because anxiety is something most people try to avoid, it's easy to see how another depression loop can get started. This is why recognizing and working on avoidance is such a crucial part of ending depression.

DEFINING AVOIDANCE

Many of the behaviors that feel right when you're depressed can serve as an avoidance or escape behavior. An escape behavior gets you out of an unpleasant situation, whereas avoidance behaviors occur after repeatedly escaping from unpleasant situations and learning to steer clear of them.

Psychologists define *avoidance* as the substitution of behaviors that bring immediate relief from distress for behaviors that may cause immediate discomfort or anxiety but can be very helpful over the long run. Avoidance may help you to temporarily escape from a difficult or painful experience. However, avoidance behaviors have no effect on or may even worsen a situation that is important and requires your attention.

Avoidance as a Natural Response to Distress

Leslie's story shows several common avoidance behaviors. You may be able to relate. Everyone procrastinates at times, and most of the time the consequences are manageable. During periods of depression, however, the process of avoidance can make it difficult to overcome depression. Part of the problem is that avoidance is a very natural process that can be extremely useful in the right situations. In other words, avoidance is a natural part of being a human being. Without it, we wouldn't be able to get ourselves out of a lot of difficult or dangerous situations.

The Flight-or-Fight Response

You may have heard of the fight-or-flight responses to danger. These are natural escape reactions to dangerous situations. You either gear up to fight—as in the case of a woman who wards off a potential purse snatcher by kicking him in the groin—or prepare to flee, as in the case of a farmhand running from a bull that has gotten loose in the pasture. Sometimes a flight response is to freeze, as in the case of a deer facing the headlights of an oncoming car at night or a person becoming mute during an intense argument.

These natural escape responses have been in the human behavioral repertoire for thousands of years. In the postindustrial world, however, people seldom need to flee from wild animals. However, people will still often avoid feelings or situations that may signal a threat. When you are depressed, many things that normally wouldn't trouble you can come to be seen as threats. For example, calling friends on the phone can raise the threat that they will not be

Checkpoint

Can you see how avoidance would be useful in your life in some situations but not others?

Yes _____ No _____

interested in talking to you or won't want to get together. Revising a resume and looking for a new job can raise the threat that you won't be able to find one. Sometimes, simply getting out of bed in the morning raises the threat that you will feel even worse if you get up. You can see how the natural tendency to avoid perceived threats can be helpful or harmful depending on the situation.

Avoidance Is Not Necessarily Intentional

When people are depressed, they typically don't say to themselves, "Well, I think I'll do everything I can to avoid things that make me uncomfortable." The process is much subtler and occurs mostly outside of your awareness. Sometimes it's so automatic that you don't even notice it. For example, during a period of mild depression, Jesse, a writer, developed a habit of checking the Internet to see how sales of a previous book were doing and then checking his e-mail several times, when he should have been sitting at the computer working on his next book, for which he had a contract. Before he knew it, Jesse was checking his e-mail ten to twenty times an hour and spending at least four hours a day on the Internet. He had a plot in mind for his new book and it was quite well developed in outline form. When he felt depressed, though, he felt disconnected from the characters and found it easier to surf the Internet. Why? When writing created distress for Jesse, checking the Internet and e-mail was a way for him to avoid the distress.

Jesse didn't develop this habit intentionally. It developed on its own because his avoidance behavior was an effective way of temporarily reducing his feelings of distress and despair about writing. The same is true with many of the avoidance strategies that you may use when you're depressed.

Exercise: Discovering Your Escape and Avoidance Behaviors

Take a moment to think back on a recent situation in which you intended to do something that you knew might have a positive impact on your depression but ended up doing just the opposite. It may have been that you were headed to meet a friend for a social engagement but instead turned back home and called to say you were feeling ill. Or, rather than completing a project, you might have spent an afternoon thinking about how low you feel.

Write the activity that you were trying to accomplish on the line below:

_____

Now, write down all of the things that seemed to get in the way of accomplishing it:

_____

_____

_____

_____

Finally, look over the list. Did any of these things make you feel relief from the need to accomplish the original task? Were they escapist activities, such as watching a television show or eating a between-meal snack? Place a check mark by all of the activities that may have served as escape or avoidance for you.

WHAT ARE YOU AVOIDING?

You may be asking, "What am I avoiding?" This question is understandable. It's often difficult to know what it is you are responding to. You may often feel fatigued and might never have considered what you were avoiding by sleeping or staying in bed.

Overwhelming Fatigue: A Way of Avoiding Uncomfortable Feelings

Fatigue is a common symptom of depression. It is natural to lie down or sleep when you feel fatigued. After a long day at work, or during the normal course of the twenty-four-hour cycle, going to bed when you feel tired is a healthy response. It is rejuvenating. However, when people are depressed, they often report that their sleep does not refresh them. In fact, they feel more tired after staying in bed. So why stay in bed? One possibility is that staying in bed is a way of avoiding all sorts of situations or feelings that you might encounter if you were to get out of bed. Consider the situation of a client named Allison.

From her activity-and-mood monitoring chart, it was clear that Allison's depression was much worse in the mornings than at any other point in her days. She would wake each morning around six-thirty and lie in bed tossing and turning for thirty minutes to an hour. Then, realizing that she needed to get ready for work, Allison would begin to ruminate about the amount of work she had to do. The stress and anxiety were so overwhelming that she often found it almost impossible to get out of bed. On such days, she would call in sick or get to work one to two hours late. Allison felt virtually no control over this pattern. As she described it, "It's just a complete rut. It sounds ridiculous, but at those times I just can't even imagine getting out of bed. The idea is too overwhelming."

What was Allison avoiding by staying in bed? There was no horrible traumatic event waiting for her. It was not physically painful to get up, and no one was there to criticize her or otherwise make her life more difficult were she to get out of bed. In fact, her life tended to go better when she did force herself to get up: she got to work earlier, completed more projects, and felt better about herself.

What Allison was avoiding was all of the thoughts, feelings, and anxieties associated with going to work. She knew that as she showered and got dressed she would worry about her appearance and think about the weight she had recently gained. She also knew that while driving to work she would play over in her mind all the possible bad things that might happen if she were not able to finish particular projects. Finally, she knew that when she arrived at work she would be hit with a wave of anxiety when she faced her desk and the many piles of papers. In the face of all of this, staying in bed provided a small amount of temporary relief, even though she was still depressed and anxious as she lay there.

Exercise: A Checklist of Avoidance Behaviors

Below is a list of situations or activities that people sometimes avoid when they are depressed and the feelings that they are avoiding. Read through the list and circle what you tend to avoid. Think about what avoidance accomplishes for you in the short term and the long term. Does it help you feel better? Does it keep you feeling safe? Does it make your depression better or worse?

Situations or Activities You May Avoid	Feelings You Are Avoiding
Potential conflicts with family, friends, or coworkers	Sadness
Difficult tasks or chores	Anger
Important tasks related to life changes (Looking for a job or a place to live, ending or beginning a relationship, etc.)	Grief
Socializing with others	Anxiety
Work	Fear
Exercise	Embarrassment
Previously enjoyable activities	Guilt

Can you think of other situations or activities you avoid?

_____

_____

_____

_____

How You Develop Avoidance Patterns.

There is an old expression, Once bitten, twice shy. This suggests that it only takes one bad experience to make you cautious in a number of similar experiences. This is how people develop avoidance patterns. Both Leslie and Allison knew from experience that going to work could be a painful experience. Allison also knew from experience that staying in bed provided some temporary relief, even though it made things more difficult in the long run. Put simply, the way she approached her mornings was a result of her past experience. She had learned that staying in bed was an effective way to cope with depression and anxiety in the short run. More generally, Allison had learned to respond to difficult situations by withdrawing rather than engaging.

This is a very common strategy when it comes to coping with difficult feelings or situations. As an example of how you can learn to withdraw rather than to engage, one psychologist (Ferster 1973) explained it like this: Imagine that a young infant cries because it is hungry. Usually, if a baby cries and is fed when it cries, it learns that crying is a form of communication that results in help from others (in the form of milk and loving care from a caregiver). Over time, the infant begins to interact with the environment and to manipulate it, so to speak, because such behaviors work. Reaching out and engaging in the world helps the infant get his or her needs met. Now imagine that people in the infant's environment do not respond when the infant reaches out by crying. This infant is less likely to learn that crying results in the removal of the difficult situation (being hungry). Instead, the baby simply cries from hunger. The infant may also suck on his or her hands as a self-soothing effort or curl into a little ball. This child is not learning to engage in the world when distressed. Instead, he or she is learning to withdraw.

Note: We are not saying that depression and avoidance are the results of bad parenting or other negative experiences in the first few months of life. The example above simply shows how learning to avoid situations can be a natural and logical response. Learning avoidance does not just happen during infancy or childhood. Adults can also learn this habit. For example, some adolescents and young adults learn that many of the anxieties and difficulties involved in interacting with peers can be avoided by drinking alcohol or using drugs. Because such behavior worked in adolescence, it can be carried into adulthood.

What's Wrong with Avoiding?

As we suggested above, in many situations avoidance is a very adaptive process, such as avoiding dark streets at night where a mugger could be lurking. But there are many other situations in which avoidance can become a problem. First, avoidance often prevents people from taking necessary steps toward solving life problems or improving their moods. For example, if you feel stuck in a bad relationship, or if there's a problem that needs solving, avoiding dealing with the issues keeps the problems alive. Avoiding sadness and grief following the loss of a loved one can prevent you from working through a natural grieving process. Or, avoiding an accumulating pile of unpaid bills can continue to produce anxiety and worry over financial difficulties, which then makes it harder to pay the bills.

Exercise: Adaptive Avoidance and Problematic Avoidance

In the two columns below list in the left-hand column situations that you avoided where the avoidance was adaptive for you. In the right-hand column, list situations where your avoidance was problematic.

Adaptive Avoidance   **Problematic Avoidance**

_____   _____

_____   _____

_____   _____

_____   _____

Avoidance can also be a problem when the very process of avoiding creates additional unpleasant feelings and experiences. This is a subtle process that is easy to experience directly with a thought experiment. For the next ten to fifteen seconds, do everything you can do to avoid imagining a pink bear. Whatever you think about, don't think about or visualize a pink bear. Try this for ten to fifteen seconds and then continue reading.

How did it work? If you're like most of us, your attempt to avoid thinking about pink bears resulted in the exact opposite: You actually spent most of the time visualizing or thinking about some sort of pink bear! It's as if the thought, "I shouldn't think about pink bears," kept reintroducing pink bears into your mind. It works the same way with avoidance of difficult experiences when you're depressed. The more effort you put into avoiding—for example, not dealing with an important piece of paperwork—the more you will worry about the paperwork.

How Do You Know If Your Behavior Is Avoidance?

Take a look back at the definition of avoidance that we provided earlier. Avoidance behavior occurs when (a) what you are doing helps you to temporarily escape from difficult situations or feelings, and (b) what you are doing fails to improve or it even worsens your depression in the long run. Now that you have had experience with activity charts and self-monitoring, you can monitor your own avoidance behaviors. To determine whether your behavior is avoidance or not, you need to look at all aspects of a situation. A behavior that is helpful in one context may be an avoidance behavior in a different context. Recall the example of Leslie setting out to clean the dishes and do laundry and ending up knitting sweaters. If, before a birthday or holiday, Leslie had set out to knit sweaters as gifts for her children, the knitting would be completely appropriate. However, in the context of needing to get housework completed, knitting was a distraction and avoidance of the discomfort of the task at hand.

The function of a behavior is also determined by its consequences. This is a fancy way of saying that behavior does not always serve the purpose that you think it does. For example, eating a piece of chocolate cake can serve many functions, depending on the situation and the consequences. If Andy, sitting at home after eating a light meal, thinks that he'd like a little taste of something sweet, and he eats a piece of chocolate cake, eating the cake functions as a nice treat that reduces his desire for a sweet. Imagine that, in a different situation, Andy is feeling badly about himself and has just eaten a large meal. He cuts himself a piece of chocolate cake out of boredom, eats it, and continues to feel dissatisfied. He also feels a little queasy. The act of eating the cake has served a very different function from the first instance. It has helped Andy to avoid boredom and has also made him feel physically ill and a little more depressed. In a different situation, Andy may be visiting a friend who offers him a piece of chocolate cake. He accepts and the two of them eat cake and drink a cup of coffee while having an interesting conversation. When he has finished eating the cake, he feels happy and connected to his friend. Eating the cake in this situation has helped to promote social interaction for Andy.

A Fail-Safe Method for Checking on Avoidance

One useful way to determine whether your behavior is helping you to avoid something is to look at circumstances and consequences.

Circumstances. What is the circumstance or situation in which the behavior occurs? Where are you? What is the time of day? Who else, if anyone, is with you? Does the situation feel difficult in any way? What is your response to the situation? What do you do in the situation?

Consequences. What are the results of the behavior? Do you feel better? Have you solved a problem? Have things remained the same? Have things gotten worse?

DEFINING A TRAP

Therapists and counselors often use particular words or acronyms to help people recognize or change behaviors. We use the acronym TRAP to help with the process of changing avoidance (first used in Martell, Addis, and Jacobson 2001). A trap is something that people can become stuck in without realizing it. In addition, each of the letters of the word "trap" points to an important part of understanding how avoidance works:

Trigger: A situation that has an impact on a person.

Response: A reaction to the trigger, frequently emotional.

Avoidance Pattern: The avoidance behavior you engage in.

Triggers for Avoidance

A *trigger* is something that sets a chain of events in motion. For example, when a traffic light turns red it is a trigger for putting your foot on the brake, thinking about stopping, and a whole collection of other small behaviors that could be called "coming to a stop." Triggers for avoidance behavior vary in many different ways. They can be historical, current, external, internal, or interpersonal. As you read about each type of trigger below, don't worry too much about remembering each one, or about being able to identify exactly into which category of trigger every event in your life falls. What's more important is that you begin to understand that there are many different types of triggers for avoidance behavior. Sometimes these triggers aren't immediately obvious without looking at them closely.

Historical Triggers

Unfortunately life does not treat everyone fairly. Many people face multiple losses, poverty, heartbreak, trauma, and other negative events that can shape who they are as adults. For some people, suffering starts early. There is a correlation, for example, between early loss and depression. If people, places, or objects associated with a loss (such as an old family picture) tend to trigger avoidance responses, then the loss is a *historical trigger*. It is historical in terms of your own personal history.

You may feel particularly bad on the anniversary of an unhappy event, like the day a loved one died. Every year, as this day approaches, you feel more and more anxious or gloomy. The association of the date with a terrible life event is painful, and the day itself takes on the characteristics of the loss. What was once simply a day of the year is now a trigger for sadness or an increase of depression symptoms. This is what we would refer to as a historical trigger. The situation is so closely associated with a painful experience in the past that it continues to influence your current behavior.

These historical events are not always as obvious as a date or a time of the year. You may have had the experience of listening to the radio and hearing a song that you have not heard in a long time and feeling blue when the song plays. Perhaps the song was a hit on the radio and you heard it frequently during a difficult period of your life; now it triggers the old feelings. We have known people who survived the horrors of Nazi concentration camps who have strong reactions to snow because they were forced to stand for hours in the snow with very little clothing as children. There are many historical triggers, and it can be difficult to know what the trigger is. It is important, however, to recognize that your mood can shift as a response to something with historical significance that you may no longer recall. In other words, the mood shift does not "come out of nowhere," although it may feel as if it does.

Current Triggers

Not all triggers have a historical context. Often, very real things can happen in the present that trigger you to avoid them. Amanda was anticipating a very difficult conversation with her partner about postponing living together. Amanda was fairly certain that her partner would be very hurt and angry about her reluctance to move in. Every time she got up in the morning and started thinking about the conversation, Amanda became sad and anxious and began puttering around the house. Amanda would feel more depressed every time she walked by the telephone or computer to call or to e-mail her partner.

In this example, there were two *current triggers* for Amanda's behavior. The first was the sight of her telephone or computer, which led Amanda to feel more depressed. The second was actually Amanda's own thinking about the conversation with her partner shortly after she got out of bed. This thinking became the trigger for all sorts of avoidance or puttering. You may have noticed that thinking is also an internal trigger, which is covered below.

External Triggers

External triggers are those that happen outside of you and have an impact on how you respond in particular situations. For example, imagine being currently depressed when your house is broken into and several important family heirlooms are taken. After dealing with the police and the insurance companies, you might become more depressed and begin to withdraw from work, friends, and family. What are the triggers here? Clearly the burglary is an external event. The loss of the family heirlooms could be a historical trigger, depending on what they were associated with in your experience, or it could be a current trigger.

Internal Triggers

Many experiences are extremely personal and private. Two people standing right next to each other in some secluded place may have very different experiences. Likewise, someone living in the middle of bustling Manhattan may keep himself or herself so distant from everyone that he or she may as well be living on a desert island. Just like the air that you breathe, your environment exists both outside of you and inside of you. Events that seem to occur more inside you are *internal triggers*. For example, some people we have worked with report having a disturbing dream and waking with a feeling of being depressed. They often don't recognize what it was about the dream that left them with this feeling, but this internal trigger, a dream, had a powerful effect on their mood. In many other cases, excessive worrying or obsessing about problems (an internal trigger) can trigger a person to avoid the tasks that will actually begin to solve the problems.

Interpersonal Triggers

Triggers can also be *interpersonal* (between people). A surly boss or coworker, a grouchy partner or spouse, or someone with a grudge against you are all people that you might wish to avoid. If, for example, your boss is very critical on a Friday, facing him or her on the following

Monday can be more difficult. In general, conflicts with children, family, or other loved ones can be powerful triggers for avoidance behavior.

Responding to Triggers

Responses to triggers are often emotional. You may be very in touch with your feelings, or you may be less so. Either way, throughout each day triggers in your environment produce emotional responses. If you drink a cup of coffee in the morning, you might feel energized or relaxed, depending on the situation. If someone you care for says something critical to you, you might feel sad, guilty, or angry. If something very positive happens, you might feel happy, hopeful, or content. This all may seem very obvious, but it's important to remember that responding emotionally to your environment is a major part of what you do all the time.

When Feelings Rule the Day

So what does this have to do with avoidance? To understand how emotional responses are linked to avoidance, you need to consider briefly the way feelings are typically talked about in Western cultures such as the United States. In this culture, a lot of importance is placed on feeling happy. There is an unwritten but powerful rule that says, "If you're feeling bad in any way, do something about it as quickly as possible, so you can get rid of the bad feelings."

Although the "get rid of bad feelings" rule works in some ways, it presents problems in other ways, and this is where avoidance comes in. The biggest problem is that it is simply impossible to get rid of a lot of difficult feelings. Responding emotionally is unavoidable. It is what people do. The second problem is that attempts to get rid of negative feelings can cause additional problems. Excessive use of alcohol or drugs, two strategies often used to cope with bad feelings, is a common example.

People often wonder what the alternative is. If you're not supposed to try to get rid of difficult or painful feelings, what should you do instead? Are you supposed to sit there and dwell in your misery? We encourage people to stop reflexively trying to get rid of bad feelings. The attempt to get rid of bad feelings operates like a reflex, almost like the way your leg kicks up automatically whenever the doctor taps on a particular spot on your knee. The goal is to stop letting what you are feeling always dictate how you will behave. Embarrassment is a good example. You might feel embarrassed if you knocked over a giant display of soup cans at the grocery store. You might want to abandon your shopping cart and run away. However, being socially responsible, you would be more likely to replace the cans on the shelf or find a clerk to assist you. This is an example of acting according to a bigger goal (being socially responsible) rather than reflexively to a feeling.

Four Facts about Responding to Triggers

Here are the important points about triggers:

1. Responses to triggers are often emotional.

2. Society encourages us to get rid of difficult or painful emotions.

3. Many attempts to get rid of bad feelings are not successful and can cause other problems.

4. An alternative is to allow yourself to feel what you feel, while continuing to act according to particular goals you have in mind.

Specific Emotional Reactions to Triggers

Below are several different types of emotional reactions. As you read about each one, try to think of instances when you've had this kind of response. You can also try to identify the situation or trigger that led to the emotional reaction that you had.

The Sadness Reaction

Sadness is one of the most common emotional reactions to depression triggers. Say you are dreading the anniversary of a loved one's death. You may take great pains to avoid the day as much as possible. Now, how do you avoid a day? It will arrive, no matter what you do. People use various strategies to avoid sadness, including sleeping, drinking, compulsive work, sex, going to the movies, and so on. Remember that these behaviors may be appropriate in some circumstances, but if you are doing any of them on the anniversary of a loved one's death, and it helps you to forget about the day and reduce some of the sadness, then the strategy functions as avoidance. Whether this avoidance is ultimately helpful or harmful to you depends on the long-term consequences of the pattern.

You might be sad if you have lost a loved one, favored possession, or prized opportunity, and

- You feel lethargic or tired.

- You have a sick feeling in your stomach.

- You have an urge to cry, whether or not you actually can cry.

- You feel flushed.

- You feel that you have lost your energy.

- You can't stop thinking about what you lost.

- You don't want to talk to anyone, or, alternatively, you have a strong urge to connect with others.

The Fear Reaction

You may not associate fear with depression. However, 60 percent of people who are depressed also suffer from an anxiety disorder. Avoidance is a key process in maintaining both anxiety and depression. You may feel very depressed and avoid certain situations because for some reason you are afraid. Avoidance keeps you from facing important things and maintains both the fear and the depression.

You may simply fear becoming more depressed. Therapists are used to hearing people who are depressed say things like, "I just can't face the day, because I know that I'm going to feel miserable and I just can't go through it again." This is an expression of fear, the fear of a feeling. Because feeling depressed is unpleasant, you can begin to fear these unpleasant feelings. You want to make them go away or to prevent them from coming. This is true in the midst of depression, when you may do whatever you can to avoid the feelings. It can also be true during periods of remission, if you become extra aware of any change in mood that might signify that you are getting depressed again.

You may be afraid if there is a perceived threat to your well-being, and

- You feel your heart rate increase.

- You notice changes in the rhythm of your breathing.

- You have a strong urge to escape.

- Your awareness of your surroundings becomes more acute.

- You cannot think as clearly as normal.

The Anger Reaction

People experience depression in different ways. Some people don't feel sad, lethargic, or fearful, but they feel irritable. Little things that are tolerable during times when they are not depressed become annoying and lead to anger. Although it can sound strange to talk of people not recognizing when they are angry, social pressures to act in civilized ways can often prevent people from recognizing when they are angry.

Some psychologists have suggested that depression is anger turned inward toward the self. Although we do not entirely agree with this view, we do recognize that it is possible, in some cases, that some of the negative thinking about yourself so common in depression may have its roots in a restriction of anger. The process can develop somewhat like this: Imagine that a child gets punished for misbehaving and feels angry. This child also has a history of being punished even more if he or she expresses anger at the parent. As a child, it may therefore be adaptive to take the anger response undercover, so to speak, to avoid further punishment. It's as if the child is saying to himself or herself, "You are bad for making Daddy mad," while at the same time feeling privately angry at the parent. By the time this child is an adult, restricting the expression of anger may have reached the level of a habit. This may also mean that people are capable of feeling angry without necessarily defining it for themselves as anger.

You know you're angry if something has happened to you that you disapprove of, and

- Your heart rate increases.

- Your face feels hot or flushed.

- Your muscles tighten.

- You clench your jaw or grit your teeth.

- Your thinking becomes focused on the perpetrator.

- You swear.

- You have an urge to attack.

Your Avoidance Patterns

The last part of the TRAP acronym refers to "avoidance pattern." Sometimes the type of avoidance you use to cope with negative feelings is so ingrained that a pattern develops. Note: You may or may not experience particular patterns of avoidance, but whether or not you do, we want you to pay attention to what you are avoiding.

What Does an Avoidance Pattern Look Like?

One of the people we worked with had learned to avoid any situation in which he needed to ask someone for help. Such situations made him anxious and his avoidance of them contained his anxiety somewhat. This man's avoidance followed a particular pattern.

Most of the time, however, human behavior is much more variable. When you say someone is shy, for example, you don't necessarily mean that he or she acts shyly all the time. Rather, you call people shy when you have seen them behave shyly so frequently that you have come to associate shy behavior with them. This is also true with avoidance. For some people, avoidance is nearly characteristic of them. For others there is no pattern.

Again, we want you to focus on your avoidance behaviors, whether or not a pattern is obvious.

Procrastination as avoidance. Procrastinating is one of the most obvious forms of avoidance. People are often aware of it when it's happening. When a task is difficult, unpleasant, or even dangerous, you may have a tendency to put it off until later. This is clear avoidance. For some people this is a habit, and procrastination is, in fact, a pattern. They leave dishes in the sink for nights on end, allow phone or e-mail messages to accumulate without responding, and have unpaid bills and uncompleted paperwork on their desks and tables. Other people only procrastinate in certain situations. Don't be fooled, however, because procrastination is a key avoidance maneuver.

Symptoms of depression as avoidance. Some of the symptoms that are characteristic of depression can function as avoidance in less obvious ways than procrastination. You may use negative thinking, for example, as a substitute for responding assertively to others. You may take the blame for things rather than confront others. Lethargy and fatigue can be a way of trying to escape or avoid the bad feelings associated with depression. Ferster (1973) described complaining as a means of avoiding a negative state. How does this work? In some circumstances, saying "I feel badly" can result in someone ministering to you. This is true for such statements as "I am thirsty or hungry," "I need some money," and so on. Now, imagine a situation when you thought "I need some money" but there was nobody around to give you any. You may worry about money or even complain to your friends about being broke (without any expectation that they'll front you a loan). When your anxiety about financial need rises to a certain level, saying (or thinking) "I need money" may bring a slight, temporary relief from the anxiety. It is as if you found an answer to the problem. In this case, the complaint serves as avoidance because it brings temporary relief but no long-term solution. The complaint may even keep you from taking the necessary steps to a reasonable solution.

Rumination as avoidance. Thinking very deeply and for long periods of time about problems can sometimes help to solve them. Other times, ruminating can be a very effective method of avoidance by helping you avoid taking difficult steps toward solving a problem. We'll have much more to say about rumination in chapter 5.

Numbing, zoning, or spacing out as avoidance. Another way people often avoid difficult emotions is by finding subtle psychological ways to not feel them. Numbing, zoning, or spacing out in front of the television, for example, can be an effective way to avoid feelings of sadness, depression, boredom, or other painful emotions. Using excessive amounts of alcohol or drugs is a less subtle but an equally effective way of avoiding emotional reactions.

RECOGNIZING TRAPS

A man is lost in the desert without food or water. He sees a bottle filled with clear liquid. The bottle says "Vodka" on it. He opens it and drinks it completely. Although there is slight burning in his throat and he coughs a little, the liquid quenches his thirst for the moment. However, he becomes more disoriented as the effects of the alcohol take hold. Furthermore, the alcohol serves to increase his dehydration. The liquid that temporarily quenched his thirst serves to hasten his death. Avoidance works the same way (Martell, Addis, and Jacobson 2001).

Sleep That's Restful and Sleep That's Not

Our depressed clients frequently complain of wanting to sleep all the time or of staying in bed for many hours each day. Sleep is natural and healthy in the normal course of a day or after you have expended a great deal of energy. When you are depressed, it can feel like the depression is taking its toll and sapping your energy. How do you know, then, when sleep is necessary for refreshment or when it is avoidance?

Again, to determine if your behavior is helping you to avoid something, you can examine the circumstances and the consequences of your behavior. In terms of circumstances, if you have been working hard at work all week, or you have had particularly taxing life experiences during the day, you may feel tired because your body needs the sleep. However, if you have averaged twelve hours of sleep for the past five nights and are in good physical health, the feeling that you need to sleep may be depression, not a true physiological need. This is the difference between feeling sleepy and feeling fatigued. The former is the normal state of having been awake for a complete period of time and needing the restorative function of sleep, and the latter is a state that is as much psychological as it is physiological.

In terms of consequences, although it is not true in every instance, you can often tell by how you feel upon waking whether sleep is avoidance. If you are in good physical health, and you sleep for seven to nine hours and awaken feeling refreshed (perhaps not immediately, but after fully waking up), then the sleep was probably necessary. If you awaken and feel tired, and just want to turn around and go back to bed, this consequence of sleep may signal that you are experiencing fatigue, not sleepiness.

Keeping Out of Harm's Way

There are many things in life that people have to face each day. Work contains some level of stress for everyone, no matter how simple your job. At other times there can be troubling life events or obnoxious individuals to face. When you are depressed, even simple tasks can seem monumental. Do you change your life so that you don't have to face things? If so, you may be stuck in an avoidance pattern. If you spend a great deal of time trying to keep away from confrontation or hassle, there are clearly situations or feelings that you are motivated to avoid.

Complaining May Be a Clue

Again, some of your symptoms can serve as avoidance. Complaining can occasionally function as avoidance—you reduce your stress or anxiety temporarily by engaging in behavior that cannot have any impact on the situation. If you find yourself complaining about things all the time, it could be a sign that you are avoiding something. There may be a more adaptive and successful way of dealing with the situation.

Exercise: Identifying TRAPs

Over the next week, see if you can identify four TRAPs that you find yourself in. An important TRAP may not feel like a big event in your life. It may happen within a few seconds or minutes, and it may not be easy to notice at first. Other TRAPs are more obvious. For each TRAP, use the worksheet below to fill in the trigger, the response, and what you are avoiding. Under "Circumstance," write down the environment or situation that you are in. Under "Consequence," write down how the avoidance pattern ultimately made you feel or other consequences it had over the next several hours or days. Before you begin, you can take a look at the following worksheet completed by a client.

TRAP Example

Circumstance: *At work before lunch on Monday.*

Trigger: *Asked coworker out for lunch, and she said she had other plans.*

Response: *Felt embarrassed, depressed.*

Avoidance Pattern: *Ate lunch alone at my desk and thought about why she wouldn't want to have lunch with me.*

Consequences: *Felt pretty depressed most of the day—avoided her for the rest of the day.*

Before you complete your own TRAP worksheet, make extra copies for future use.

TRAP Worksheet

Instructions: Fill in the blanks for four different TRAPs that you find yourself in.

TRAP 1

Circumstance: _____

Trigger: _____

Response: _____

Avoidance Pattern: _____

Consequences: _____

TRAP 2

Circumstance: _____

Trigger: _____

Response: _____

Avoidance Pattern: _____

Consequences: _____

TRAP 3

Circumstance: _____

Trigger: _____

Response: _____

Avoidance Pattern: _____

Consequences: _____

TRAP 4

Circumstance: _____

Trigger: _____

Response: _____

Avoidance Pattern: _____

Consequences: _____

What did you notice from the TRAP worksheet? Were some TRAPs easier to recognize than others? You may want to carry little TRAP cards with you that you can fill out whenever you notice a particular avoidance pattern happening. The more you can increase your awareness of TRAPs, the easier it is to get out of them, which is the next step.

HOW TO GET BACK ON TRAC

Sometimes becoming more aware of your TRAPs is enough to help you change some of them. After all, if you don't understand the subtle ways that avoidance may be making your depression worse, or at least making it more difficult to overcome, then you aren't in a position to get out of TRAPs. The most straightforward way to get out of a TRAP is to get back on TRAC, an acronym we've developed (first used in Martell, Addis, and Jacobson 2001) that stands for

Trigger: Same trigger as the TRAP.

Response: The same feeling that you have in the TRAP.

Alternative Coping: An active, rather than avoidant, response.

Finding the Alternative

Figuring out how to get back on TRAC requires you to find alternative ways to cope with the same triggers and responses that occur in a TRAP. These alternative coping strategies are active, rather than avoidant, responses. The idea of blocking avoidance patterns and finding alternative coping is relatively new to self-activation treatment for depression, although the negative impact of avoidance has been recognized for years (Ferster 1973). Behaviorists treating depression have created procedures that block avoidance without emphasizing avoidance as a problem (Lewinsohn 1974). Blocking avoidance has been used with some success in the treatment of anxiety disorders (Barlow 1988).

How to Cope with Fears

Avoidance is a key factor in anxiety disorders. The treatment for many such fear-related disorders is called *exposure*. Exposure simply means facing something that you either fear or find distressing in some other way. A person who is afraid of dogs, for example, would be doing exposure if he or she stroked a dog. Exposure can be done in an intensive way. For example, the person with a fear of dogs could go to the pound and pet as many dogs as possible, especially the large or scariest-looking ones. This is also called *flooding*. Exposure can also be done in a graduated fashion. The same person might start out watching television shows about dogs. He or she would then come within the same vicinity as a puppy or small dog and eventually pet or hold a puppy or small dog. Ultimately, he or she would learn to approach large and formerly "scary" dogs.

In our approach to self-activation, we encourage people to take this more graduated approach. The reason for this is that when you're depressed you are already more likely to feel overwhelmed and incapable of completing tasks or facing situations. If you expect yourself to do the most difficult task right off the bat, avoidance is more likely. So we encourage you to set yourself up for success by taking a more gradual approach.

The rest of this book focuses on helping you get back on TRAC. You can take a graduated approach, and eventually you will be facing challenges that you thought you could not face. You may, however, also want to challenge your habitual style. If you have taken on big tasks in the past that resulted in disappointing results, slow down, and take much smaller steps. If you tend to be timid and try only the safest changes, you might want to push yourself a little. You can use your own style or challenge yourself with this book. Steady forward movement is what counts.

TRAC Worksheet

You can make copies of this worksheet for future use. For each circumstance in which you have identified a TRAP, fill in the information that will help you get back on TRAC. Using the same circumstances, triggers, and responses from your TRAP worksheet, write down several possible alternative coping behaviors to break the avoidance pattern. Then choose one alternative and commit to a time to try it. Once you've tried the alternative behavior observe the consequences and continue to use this method with other alternatives.

TRAC

Circumstance: _____

Trigger: _____

Response: _____

Possible Alternative Coping Behaviors: _____

_____

_____

Choose One Alternative to Try: _____

_____

Commit to a time to try it: _____

Consequences: _____

Self-Soothing as Alternative Coping

We want to stress that there are times when people need a break and can choose not to approach or face a distressing situation. Although we encourage you to act according to your goals, values, or commitments, rather than let your feelings control your behavior, we also recognize that there are times in life when everyone needs comfort. Sometimes lying in bed and crying can be a way to soothe yourself during a time of distress. Self-soothing strategies can be part of good self-care. In fact, self-soothing may be a way to get back on TRAC if you don't tend to nurture yourself.

Self-soothing can therefore be a positive behavior. But it's also important to know that there are healthy and unhealthy ways to soothe yourself.

Rule of thumb for self-soothing. Self-soothing behaviors provide a sense of calm, or give pleasure in the midst of emotional pain. They do not completely remove the pain, but they allow you to have temporary respite while still allowing the experience without avoidance.

Self-soothe, don't anesthetize. There is a fine line between doing things that provide solace and trying to block out pain. Self-soothing is about taking care of yourself. Anesthesia is for blocking pain. In medicine, anesthesia either numbs a part of your body or renders you unconscious. Although there may be times in life when you would like to be knocked out in order to escape from emotional suffering, it is never a healthy thing to do. Just like general anesthesia, things that knock you out also render you incapable of basic functioning and can have long-term side effects and negative consequences.

Some more adaptive ways to self-soothe include

- taking a warm bath

- going for a walk

- having coffee or some other drink with friends

- watching a movie or television program

- listening to enjoyable music

- working out or playing a sport

- gardening

- working on an enjoyable project

There are many other ways to self-soothe not included on this list. Ultimately, you are the best judge of what helps you feel better temporarily without reinforcing an avoidance pattern. Like everything else, a little bit of experimenting goes a long way.

Exercise: Monitoring TRAPs and Getting on TRAC during the Week

Continue to monitor the TRAPs you find yourself in over the next week. For each one, consider at least two alternative coping strategies that might get you back on TRAC. Then, try one out and observe the effects. How did you feel at the time? What were the short-term (within an hour) and long-term (over the next several days) consequences?

CHAPTER SUMMARY

Avoidance is a major part of the process that maintains depression. Increasing your awareness of avoidance and taking steps to overcome it are critical steps in the path to ending depression. Avoidance happens when behaviors help you to temporarily avoid or escape from difficult or painful situations or feelings. However, these same behaviors have no effect on or tend to worsen a situation that is important and requires your attention. The process of avoidance is often subtle and can be understood as a TRAP. This acronym describes avoidance as consisting of a trigger, a response, and an avoidance pattern. To get out of TRAPs, you will need to develop alternative coping strategies. This means learning how to respond actively to situations or feelings that make you uncomfortable. The rest of this workbook shows you exactly how to work through this process.

Chapter 4

Take ACTION: First Steps toward Change

The first three chapters of this workbook were designed to help you develop a solid understanding of depression and how it operates in your particular situation. At this point, it's a good idea to stop and consider what you've learned about your own depression so far. Below are some thoughts that a client named Stephanie wrote down after considering how her depression works:

- "I'm often not aware of the patterns I get into that keep me depressed."

- "Nighttime is the hardest part of the day."

- "I spend a lot of time worrying about things and being self-critical."

- "I seem to feel better when I'm at work, as long as I'm not talking to my boss."

- "My mood goes up and down more than I realized."

- "I avoid spending time with friends and family because I don't want to feel awkward around them when I'm depressed."

Exercise: What Have You Learned So Far?

You may have learned some things similar to those that Stephanie learned. If so, put a check mark by those comments that reflect how you feel too. In the space below, you can write down other facts you've learned about your depression.

1. _____

_____

2. _____

_____

3. _____

_____

4. _____

_____

5. _____

_____

PREPARING FOR CHANGE

Now that you've learned a bit about how your depression works, it's time to start making some changes. Change is not always easy, but it doesn't always have to be hard, either. It helps to go about change in the right way. Here are some ideas to keep in mind as you begin to make changes:

- Keep a curious and open mind about the changes you're making.

- Treat changes in your behavior as experiments from which you can learn rather than as tests of your willpower or self-worth.

- To maximize the likelihood of success, choose new behaviors that are manageable.

- Don't take on too much at once or raise your expectations too high.

- Separate the process of making changes into steps.

- Avoid criticizing, shaming, or blaming yourself as you make changes.

- "Just do it" just doesn't work. If change were that easy, you would have done it already.

Over many years of working with depression, we have seen countless examples of positive changes in people's lives. Change is always possible if you go about it in the right way. That's what the rest of this book is all about: guiding you through changes in your behavior in ways that work for you. Before getting started, though, let's take a closer look at Stephanie's situation.

Stephanie's Evenings

One of the things Stephanie learned about her depression was that nighttime was the hardest part of the day. Her typical pattern involved getting home from work around six-thirty, pouring herself a glass of wine, and sitting down in front of the television. By eight o'clock she was typically feeling hungry but too tired to prepare anything. Stephanie usually heated up a high-calorie frozen dinner and ate in front of the television. She would sit on the couch feeling guilty about her poor eating habits until she drifted off to sleep, typically waking around midnight and going to bed.

Stephanie's First Steps toward Change

Stephanie decided to try making some changes in her evening routine. She made a commitment to changing three behaviors.

Rather than . . .	She would . . .
Watching television from six-thirty until eight o'clock at night	Read, take a walk, or do some chores around the house
Eating a frozen dinner	Cook herself something she enjoyed, or make plans to have dinner with a friend
Falling asleep in front of the television	Watch up to one hour of television before bed without falling asleep on the couch (and set a cooking timer for one hour in case she dozed off)

Stephanie decided to try these new behaviors on Monday, Tuesday, and Wednesday of the following week. She also made a commitment to pay close attention to how she felt during and after each new experience so that she could see the results of her experiment. As you might expect, Stephanie found that her mood improved greatly when she made these changes. Although she had occasional relapses, she knew it when they happened, and rather than falling into habits that put her at risk for depression, she became better at choosing how she wanted to spend her evenings.

Checkpoint

When you're depressed, do you often feel like you're reacting automatically to situations rather than actively choosing how you want to respond?

Yes _____ No _____

THE POWER OF ACTION

After reading about Stephanie's changes, you're probably thinking, "Right. It's easy to change. Just make a plan and do it." Is it that easy? The answer is, yes and no. Yes, change is all about making a plan, following it, and seeing what happens. On the other hand, it's not always easy to know what sort of plan to make, how to follow through with it, or how to know if it worked. That's why we are not saying that you should just do it. If it were that easy, you would have already made the changes!

Over the years, we have developed a method for beginning to make changes in depressive habits based on the acronym ACTION (first used in Martell, Addis, and Jacobson 2001). This term breaks down the process of making changes into manageable steps that keep you on track and help you follow through with your plans. Here's what ACTION is all about:

A = Assess your mood and behavior.

C = Choose alternative behaviors.

T = Try out the alternatives.

I = Integrate these changes into your life.

O = Observe the results.

N = Now evaluate.

The N can also stand for "never give up." In other words, keep trying this method again and again, because positive change often takes time. The rest of this chapter is about putting ACTION into action. Here are the steps.

Assess Your Mood and Behavior

To assess something is to take a close look at it. When you assess your own behavior, as you did in the first three chapters, you develop a deeper, more precise understanding of what you're doing and how it's working. Assessing your behavior is something you should do on a regular basis (several times a day, at least) when you're working on ending depression. You can assess your behavior at any given moment by asking yourself the following questions:

1. What am I doing right now?

2. How am I feeling?

3. Do I need to make any changes in what I'm doing or how I'm doing it?

You can also assess your behavior over several days or weeks to detect regular patterns or habits that need to be changed.

Daniel's Assessment of His Depression

Daniel had become depressed following a divorce and the loss of a custody battle over his son, Charlie. Daniel's ex-wife lived within fifteen miles of him, yet he only had visitation rights to see Charlie every other weekend. Daniel had a housemate named Daphne. Although they were just friends and housemates now, Daniel and Daphne had had a brief affair just prior to Daniel's separation from his wife. In fact, it was when his wife had discovered that Daniel was having multiple affairs that she filed for divorce.

Daphne was a great housemate. However, her presence reminded Daniel of the mistake he had made by having affairs, which had cost him his marriage.

Once a week, Daniel visited a psychologist for treatment of depression. After he completed three weeks of activity monitoring charts, Daniel and his therapist noticed some consistent patterns. With the exception of one weekend during which Charlie visited, Daniel was sad, angry, or irritated when he was at home. At work, he was relieved, content, and recorded feeling upbeat. There was one problem, however. Since he had been feeling depressed, Daniel would miss entire days of work, staying at home in bed or on the sofa watching The Weather Channel or old Westerns on television. Daniel's assessment contained the following information:

Situation	Problem Behavior(s)	Feelings/Moods
1. Weekday mornings	Lying in bed for several hours	Sad, depressed, angry

Exercise: Making Your Assessment

Now take a look back at the activity-and-mood monitoring charts you completed in chapter 2. Also consider how you've been feeling and what you've been doing over the past three or four days. What patterns do you notice? Which behaviors in which situations are making your depression worse? What are some behaviors and situations that you would like to change and that you feel reasonably confident about changing? Below is a space for you to complete an assessment similar to the one that Daniel completed.

Situation	Problem Behavior(s)	Feelings/Moods
1.		
2.		

Common Problem Behavior(s)

If you have trouble identifying problem behavior, below are some behaviors that people often try to change in order to overcome depression:

- inactivity (lying around too much, watching television)

- lack of assertiveness at work or at home

- worrying or spending lots of time thinking self-critical thoughts

- repeated conflicts or arguments with others

- too much time spent doing work or chores and not enough relaxation and fun

Problems Assessing?

Here are some issues you may run into when working on assessing behaviors to change.

Difficulty defining your problem behaviors. Make sure that you define the problem clearly, without being too vague or general. For example, "being lazy" could mean sitting on the couch weekday evenings from 6:30 to 8:30 P.M. Or it could mean avoiding paying bills and returning phone calls on the weekends. "Overeating" could mean eating meal portions that are too large. Or it could mean eating too much high-fat or high-calorie food. "Spending too much time by myself" could mean avoiding contacting friends to get together. Or it could mean turning down invitations to social gatherings. So be as specific as you can.

Difficulty identifying patterns or problem behaviors. You need to pay close attention to the patterns or habits that are making it harder to end depression. You may need to start monitoring your activities and moods more frequently. It's easy to lose sight of your own behavior and slip into patterns of which you are unaware.

Difficulty identifying the situation in which the behavior occurs. Sometimes it may seem as if the behaviors you want to change are everywhere. For example, if you would like to act with greater self-confidence, you might have the sense that you lack self-confidence in many different areas of life. Even if a problem behavior occurs in many different situations, it's best to focus on changing it in one particular situation. For example, it might help to start by focusing on acting more self-confidently when presenting your ideas to other people at work.

Feeling hopeless or pessimistic about the possibility of change. These feelings are much more likely to be symptoms of depression than good reflections of how things will turn out. Yes, it is unlikely (although possible) that one specific change will end your depression. In doing this work, you will undoubtedly learn something and, at the very least, you will have begun to take action in your life. Change is often a gradual process that requires some patience and curiosity.

Checkpoint

Have you been able to identify specific problem behaviors that are making it harder to end depression?

Yes _____ No _____

If you are still having difficulty identifying specific problem behaviors, don't worry too much about it. Go back to the activity-and-mood monitoring charts and use them to schedule activities during your week. If you find that you are not accomplishing certain planned tasks, this is your cue that there may be a TRAP. Even if you can't identify the trigger, try to assess if the way you have approached the task is serving you well or not. This is all you need do to start identifying problem behaviors.

Choose Alternative Behaviors

Choosing is about selecting new ways of approaching situations, so you can try them out as replacements for existing problem behaviors. It's also about being aware at any given time that you have choices, no matter how small or how few. The goal is to choose how to respond to situations rather than to respond to situations reflexively, out of habit. Below you can see how making choices became so important in Daniel's situation.

Daniel's Choices

Daniel and his therapist discussed his dilemma. They recognized that staying at home in the mornings actually blocked Daniel's chance of feeling better and having some relief from his depression. Daniel knew that if he went to work he'd feel better. However, when he woke up feeling groggy, sad, and hopeless, he usually thought the only way to feel better was to stay in bed all day. This was a TRAP for Daniel, and he recognized that staying in bed was a choice, as was getting up and going to work, falling back asleep, or doing any one of a number of other things.

His psychologist suggested that Daniel ask himself each morning whether or not he wanted to feel better and have a sense of accomplishment. If the answer was yes, Daniel knew that he could achieve it by going to work, and that staying home would have the opposite effect. If he chose to stay home, Daniel agreed to make a note to himself, acknowledging that he was deciding to take a break from his therapy goals and deciding to allow himself to feel depressed. For Daniel, just recognizing this pattern, acknowledging that he could change his mood significantly by going to work, allowed him to get to work nearly every morning. This was a minor breakthrough for Daniel in ending his depression.

Here was how Daniel documented his situation and wrote down his alternatives. He used a scale of 1 to 5 to rate how difficult and how helpful he thought each option would be.

Situation: *Waking up feeling depressed on a weekday morning and trying to decide whether to go to work*

Behavior to change: *Staying in bed and calling in sick to work*

Option A: *Get out of bed, read the newspaper, and decide during breakfast whether I want to go to work*

Difficulty: *3 (somewhat difficult)*

Helpfulness: *2 (a little helpful)*

Option B: *Get out of bed, get ready, and go to work without allowing myself the possibility of staying home*

Difficulty: *3 (somewhat difficult)*

Helpfulness: *5 (very helpful)*

Writing down his alternatives helped Daniel reach his goals. Writing down your alternatives can help you too.

Different Types of Choices

Now it's time to choose an alternative behavior to try in place of the problem behavior you've identified in each situation. It's important to remember that your choices don't need to be heroic. Expecting yourself to make changes that are well beyond your current abilities can be a setup for failure. Instead, choose an alternative behavior that is within your reach in terms of difficulty and has a reasonable chance of being helpful. Place a star next to the option you've chosen for each problem behavior.

Exercise: What Are Your Choices?

Take a look at the assessment of your behaviors that you would like to change. Select at least two that you feel reasonably confident you could change. Write down the situations and behaviors in the spaces provided below. Then, for each behavior, think of as many possible alternative behaviors as you can and write them down as options. Don't worry about results right now. At this point, you're simply thinking of alternatives. Once you have a number of alternatives for each behavior, write down how difficult each one would be. Use a scale of 1 (not at all difficult) to 5 (extremely difficult). Then estimate how helpful the alternative is likely to be in shifting your mood in a positive direction. Again, use a scale of 1 (not at all helpful) to 5 (extremely helpful).

1. Situation: _____

Behavior to change: _____

Option A: _____

Difficulty (1–5): _____

Helpfulness (1–5): _____

Option B: _____

Difficulty (1–5): _____

Helpfulness (1–5): _____

Option C: _____

Difficulty (1–5) : _____

Helpfulness (1–5): _____

2. Situation: _____

Behavior to change: _____

Option A: _____

Difficulty (1–5): _____

Helpfulness (1–5): _____

Option B: _____

Difficulty (1–5): _____

Helpfulness (1–5): _____

Option C: _____

Difficulty (1–5): _____

Helpfulness (1–5): _____

Difficulties Choosing?

Here are some reasons that you may have difficulty choosing alternative behaviors.

Your choices are not well-defined. Make sure that your options are clearly spelled out. For example, rather than writing down "be more optimistic" as an alternative to avoiding looking for a new job, consider an option like "spend thirty minutes each morning reading the want ads and revising my resume." When alternative behaviors are vaguely defined, they are much harder to do and have a lower likelihood of being helpful.

Fear of failing. Some concern about failing is a natural response to trying any new behavior. If you find yourself paralyzed by fear or anxiety, perhaps the difficulty level of the option you chose is too high. If the difficulty level isn't too high, perhaps you're avoiding making changes out of habit. When depression has been with you for a while, it can be especially hard to get going on any changes. You may feel stuck, or you may have lost your confidence that you can actually feel better. In either case, it helps to remember that taking ACTION is not a test of your willpower or self-worth. You're doing this to learn what helps you combat depression.

Try Out the Alternatives

Pick a particular time to try out each alternative behavior you've chosen. Plan on trying out each new behavior at least three times before forming an impression of its effects on your mood. Making a written commitment to a behavioral change usually increases the likelihood of following through. In fact, research shows that making written or other public commitments increases the odds of follow-through (Norcross and Vangarelli 1988).

Exercise: Writing It Down

Below is a space for you to make a written commitment if you would like to do so.

I _____ commit to _____

during the times of _____ on the following days

and dates: _____ .

Signed, _____

Daniel's Experiments with Change

On the first morning, Daniel followed through with his plan to ask himself if he wanted to feel better that day and have a sense of accomplishment. He decided that he did and, as planned, he went to work. Once at work for an hour or so, Daniel noticed that his mood was pretty good. The depression was not completely gone, but he noticed that he felt much better than the previous week and was spending much less time worrying and feeling guilty. Virtually the same thing happened on the second day.

On the third day, Daniel woke up feeling very depressed. He couldn't imagine going to work, but he remembered his commitment to change. So he asked himself if he wanted to feel better that day and have a sense of accomplishment. In fact, he decided that although he did want to feel better, he still did not want to go to work. He decided to stay home from work even though he knew he might be more depressed as a result. Interestingly, a couple of hours after making the decision, Daniel realized that he felt awful, but that this feeling didn't come out of nowhere. He knew that his decision not to do the very thing that might make him feel better was contributing to his bad mood. As a result, he went to work for the second half of the day and felt much better.

Change Can Feel Awkward

It may feel awkward to try a new behavior. This is to be expected. Changing behavior that has become a habit is a bit like crossing your arms in a different direction. Try crossing your arms right now. Now, reverse your arms so that the one that was on top is now on the bottom, and vice versa. Pretty awkward feeling isn't it? But if you kept at it a few more times, the new way would feel familiar. It's the same way with behavioral changes when you're depressed. You should expect things to feel a little awkward, but try not to let the feeling get in the way of your following through on your experiment.

Integrate These Changes into Your Life

Repeat your experiments. Unless the results of trying particular new behaviors are disastrous, it's a good idea to try the behavior at least three times before deciding how helpful it is. Don't rely on information you get from one or even two tries. Imagine that you decide to exercise for an hour three times a week. On your first scheduled day, you go to the gym, walk in the door, and right in front of you stands an ex-lover you haven't seen since a very painful breakup a few years ago. Understandably, your time spent exercising will probably not be very relaxing, although it could be. If you gave up exercising because of the bad experience, you would lose out on what could be a great change in the long run. The point is that factors beyond your control can sometimes have an impact on the helpfulness of any new behavior.

The Power of Routines

Another reason to repeat new behaviors several times has to do with the power of routines. A routine is different than a rut. Routines are patterns of behavior that occur at regular times, such as eating, sleeping, going to work, exercising, and so on. Research has shown that regular disruptions in daily routines can place some people at risk for mood disorders like depression (Ehlers, Frank, and Kupfer 1988). It appears that people function best when their daily activities are in sync with regular cues from the environment, such as the passage of time, changes in light, and so on.

The Power of Practice

If you've ever tried to take up a new hobby or sport, you know that practice matters. When you learn a new skill, you have to accept the awkwardness of trying new things and continue to work on improving. It might sound strange, but the same is true for practicing new ways to respond to a depressed mood. For example, if you tend to respond to your depression by drinking alcohol, it will feel awkward the first time you try gardening, listening to music, or socializing instead. If you stop after trying once, you'll never know how helpful these new behaviors could have been.

Difficulties Integrating Changes?

Here are some obstacles you may face as you begin integrating the new behaviors into your daily life.

Too many changes. You may find that you're trying to make too many new changes right off the bat. Start slowly, but make a commitment. Ask yourself, "What's a manageable change that I can integrate into my life as an experiment over the next week?" Then, commit to making the change and seeing what happens. Quality is more important than quantity. You can learn a great deal from planning, committing to, and following through on one important change. If you try to do too much, you'll probably have a hard time following through on anything.

Trouble following through. If you're having trouble following through on these changes, then you need to identify what the obstacles are. Is it fear? Avoidance? Hopelessness about the possibility of change? If fear, anxiety, or pessimism about the future is getting you stuck, review the earlier discussion on difficulties choosing.

It may be that something else is keeping you stuck. Sometimes your life may be so complicated that you lose track of time and forget what you've planned on doing. If this is the case, simple written reminders in obvious places or phone or e-mail messages to yourself can be helpful.

Observe the Results

Now it's time to see what you're learning from your experiments with taking ACTION. When you try a new behavior, take a moment to assess how your mood is a few minutes to an hour beforehand. Then, make a quick note of how you feel during the experiment and your mood directly after it's over. Also, consider how you feel the remainder of the day or the next morning. Don't spend a great deal of time trying to figure out how you feel. Just do a quick check-in with yourself and then focus your attention on what you're doing.

Daniel's Observations

Daniel reported that he learned a great deal by observing how new behaviors affected his mood. Below is a form that he filled out that describes one thing he observed. In addition to seeing the positive effects of going to work in the morning, Daniel also observed that he felt anxious while lying in bed. Daniel had never realized this before because he had assumed that his mood only shifted back and forth between depressed and happy. Recognizing his anxiety led Daniel to use some simple coping techniques, such as deep breathing, to help him get out of bed in the morning.

Date	Situation	Mood/Feelings (Before)	New Behavior	Mood/Feelings (After)
5/3/03	Lying in bed Monday morning	Depressed, anxious, just sort of blah	Get up quickly, prepare for work, and leave for work	Much better, a little proud of myself for doing it, somewhat hopeful

Now Evaluate

You've now taken yourself through the process of taking ACTION. It's time to evaluate how it went. Here are some questions you should consider:

- Did the new behaviors help to improve your mood? If not, why?

- Did you have difficulty following through?

- Did you follow through but find that other options were more helpful?

- Do you want to continue with the routine you developed during the experiment?

- What have you learned overall from this experiment?

Checkpoint

Do you see value in taking ACTION as a way to help end depression?

Yes _____ No _____

Are you willing to try taking ACTION in your life on a daily basis?

Yes _____ No _____

Exercise: What Are Your Observations?

Below is a chart similar to the one Daniel filled out. You can use it to jot down some notes on what you observed during your experiments.

Date	Situation	Mood/Feelings (Before)	New Behavior	Mood/Feelings (After)

Never give up—apply the steps of ACTION repeatedly. You may choose to change the alternative behaviors you've worked on for a variety of reasons, but keep trying out new behaviors. When you're depressed, it is tempting to give up quickly, because it is hard to put the effort in. However, you can see how the process of taking ACTION is really a *series* of experiments. With each one, you will learn something new about the links between your behavior and your mood.

TAKE ACTION DAY TO DAY, HOUR TO HOUR, AND MOMENT TO MOMENT

Taking action applies to more than experiments that take place over several days or weeks. It is also possible to take action moment to moment, hour to hour, and day to day in your life. If this sounds a little fluffy, here's what we mean practically: At any point in time, remember that you are choosing to do what you're doing, and you have options.

It's very easy to forget that you have choices. At times, you may feel that you have no options at all. For example, if you're currently working at a job that you don't like, but you need money to pay the bills, you may feel stuck in this position. When you're sitting at your desk thinking about all the reasons you don't like your job, you may think you have no alternatives. In fact, it might not be wise to quit your job at this point. However, and this is a big however, you do have choices about your own behavior in each moment. Take the moment we just described. As you sit at your desk, one option is to think about all the things you don't like about your job. Another option is to look out the window (if you have one) and observe what you see. Another option is to tackle whatever project is in front of you, which may take your mind off your situation.

This is not to say that everyone is free to do whatever they want with their lives whenever they want to do it. Clearly, there are some limits on personal freedom. However, when you're feeling depressed, one of the first things you begin to lose is your sense of choice. Taking action is a powerful way to get it back.

CHAPTER SUMMARY

This chapter covered ways you can begin to regain control of your life by taking ACTION. Taking ACTION requires that you first assess how your behaviors and your moods are linked. Then, you need to choose alternative behaviors to replace those that are making it difficult to end depression. Next, you need to try out new behaviors by integrating them into your daily life. Observing the results can then let you know how helpful a new behavior is. Then you evaluate how your experiment went. What did you learn? What changes in your behavior do you wish to keep? Taking action is a powerful way to combat depression day to day, hour to hour, and moment to moment.

Chapter 5

Stop Worrying about Your Inner Child and Develop Your Outer Adult

During the 1980s, many popular self-help books, motivational speakers, and television and radio talk shows began focusing on the importance of the "inner child." Essentially, the idea was that inside each of us, psychologically speaking, there is a little child who has suffered a series of emotional wounds while growing up. The key to happiness as an adult is to get to know this child by focusing on your innermost thoughts and feelings, and from where they might come. According to this notion, if something bothers you, you must get in touch with your deepest feelings about it to figure out how your inner child is playing a role in the problem.

Of course, the idea that your experiences as a child can affect who you are as an adult is nothing new. In some ways, this idea has been the backbone of psychology since Freud. But, then again, the recent focus on the "inner child" reflects a problem with how people are often encouraged to cope with experiences like depression. What's the problem? In a nutshell, thinking deeply about who you are, what you're feeling, and what might be causing it isn't always helpful. In fact, doing so can often be harmful if your goal is to overcome depression (Nolen-Hoeksema, Parker, and Larson 1994).

HOW WORRY WORKS

When Larry began self-activation therapy, he had already read several books and listened to numerous talk shows and news programs about depression. Larry was convinced that he had low self-esteem as a result of a difficult childhood. He had also begun recording his dreams each night and trying to understand what they might be telling him about why he was depressed. Larry spent most of his time driving to and from work thinking about what might have happened to him as a child and how it affected his mind. Although he had occasional glimpses of understanding, the more he thought about things, the less clear it seemed. And the more he thought about things, the more depressed he felt.

What went wrong? Why wasn't it helpful for Larry to analyze himself in such detail? Isn't the best way to overcome depression to understand what's happening in your mind? The answer is, yes and no. As we said, it can be helpful to think deeply about yourself, but it can also be harmful. The purpose of this chapter is to help you tell the difference so that you can choose what you want to do in particular situations.

WHAT YOU'RE THINKING ABOUT VS. WHY YOU'RE THINKING

Psychologists often make a distinction between the content of your thinking and its function. The content is what you're thinking *about*. For example, below are some things that you may think about when you're feeling depressed. Place a check mark in the box next to each one that seems relevant to you:

☐   "I've failed in so many different things in my life."

☐   "I don't like myself very much and I wish I were different."

☐   "I feel guilty or ashamed of things I've done in the past."

☐   "I wish I could just escape from this all."

☐   "I'm so depressed, I can't snap out of it."

☐   "My life has been one series of disappointments."

☐   "I've gotten a raw deal."

Many therapies for depression focus on trying to change the content of your thinking, or what you think about when you're depressed. Our approach to ending depression is a bit different when it comes to thinking. We want you to focus on the function of your thinking, or *why* you're thinking at any particular time. After all, thinking is only one sort of activity you could be doing in any particular situation. You could be doing something else, so why are you thinking? Below are some examples of different functions of thinking. Place a check mark next to the functions of thinking that seem relevant to you:

- ☐ You think about why you're depressed to try to figure it out and solve the problem.

- ☐ You think about painful feelings and situations while lying in bed (rather than getting up and starting your day).

- ☐ You worry about something bad happening in the future as a way to avoid focusing on what's happening right now.

- ☐ You hold onto bad feelings about people or situations from the past because letting go of them will let those who have hurt you off the hook.

If this seems like it's getting a little complicated, here's the bottom line: It isn't always necessary to try to change what you're thinking about when you're depressed, nor do you need to get into arguments with yourself about thinking more positively or less negatively. What you need to do is understand what thinking is doing for you at any particular time. Is it helping you to feel less depressed? Are you even aware that you're doing it? What else could you be doing? This approach to your own thinking will become even clearer as you learn about a particular type of thinking that's very common among people who are depressed.

WHAT DO COWS KNOW ABOUT DEPRESSION? THE POWER OF RUMINATION

Over the last decade, researchers in psychology have identified a particular type of human activity that is consistently linked to depressed mood. This activity is called *ruminating*. The word comes from a Latin term that describes how cows chew their cud. In psychology, it refers to the activity of dredging up and turning over bad things that have happened in the past, painful thoughts and feelings, and troubling worries.

Rumination is a word that covers a lot of different types of behaviors. Here are some other behaviors that are similar to ruminating. Put a check mark next to the behaviors that you have observed yourself doing when you feel depressed:

- ☐ worrying

- ☐ overanalyzing or overthinking things

- ☐ obsessing

- ☐ brooding

- ☐ turning a problem over and over in your mind

- ☐ racking your brain about problems

- ☐ stewing about a problem for long periods of time

Overcoming the Rumination Habit

This chapter will show you how rumination operates and why it's a problem. It will then provide step-by-step guides to overcoming rumination and ending depression. First, take a few moments and consider what sorts of things you tend to turn over and over in your mind. Some common things that people ruminate about include:

- relationship problems or breakups

- hurts and disappointments suffered in the past

- worries about the future

- financial difficulties

- bad decisions made in the past

- painful feelings such as sadness, guilt, or shame

- what others think of you

Exercise: What Are Your Rumination Topics?

As you move through this chapter, you will become more and more expert on your own particular type of ruminating. For now, write down several things that lead you to ruminate. If you're not sure whether you ruminate about a particular issue, put a question mark next to it.

1. _____

2. _____

3. _____

4. _____

5. _____

6. _____

7. _____

Take a look at your list of rumination topics. What do you notice? Are there some topics about which you ruminate that make you feel more depressed than others? Is there a theme or pattern to your rumination? Or are there several different things that prompt you to ruminate?

Exercise: What Emotions or Thoughts Occur When You Ruminate?

Consider how you feel when you ruminate about these different issues. In the space below, write down several emotions or thoughts that occur when you ruminate about particular topics. You might want to consult the list of feeling words in chapter 2.

1. _____

_____

2. _____

_____

3. _____

_____

4. _____

_____

5. _____

_____

6. _____

_____

Take a look at your list of emotions. What are the most common feelings you experience when you ruminate? What sorts of thoughts go through your mind? Does it depend on the particular topic about which you're ruminating?

Ruminating Makes Your Mood Worse

Several research studies have shown that when people are encouraged to ruminate their mood worsens (Lyubomirsky and Tkach 2003). Imagine that you were asked to fill out a brief questionnaire about your mood at a particular time during the day. Now, imagine that just after completing the questionnaire, you were instructed to think deeply for several minutes about something in your life that troubles you. After several minutes of ruminating, you stop and complete the same mood questionnaire. What do you think would be the results of this small thought experiment? In all likelihood, your mood would get worse. Of course, this is probably not a huge surprise. You probably know from experience that ruminating can worsen your mood. However, if you're like most people, you are not always aware that you're ruminating. Even if you are, it can seem very difficult to stop.

Checkpoint

Does your mood tend to get worse or stay negative when you ruminate about problems?

Yes _____ No _____

Ruminating Makes You Less Willing and Able to Solve Problems

A depressed client named Bill once related a story in which his car broke down on the side of the highway. Bill assumed that he had run out of gas and was so angry at himself about this that he sat in his car and stewed for ten minutes over his own forgetfulness ("I should have known better. Now I'll be late and catch hell from my boss"). Out of anger, Bill finally slammed open the hood of the car and stared inside. After a few seconds, he noticed that one of the battery cables was loose. After quickly retightening it, he was back on the road. In the meantime, Bill's ruminating had made him ten minutes later to work than he would have been if he had simply checked under the hood right away.

Bill's experience is not unusual. Research has shown that when people ruminate, they are less able to solve problems. One well-known study showed that when people ruminate they focus on their problems in a self-critical way. They also lack self-confidence and have reduced optimism about the future. When people ruminate in this way, they are also less willing to solve their problems (Lyubomirsky et al. 1999). Does this sound like Bill or anyone you know?

Checkpoint

Do you find it difficult to actively solve problems when you're worrying intensely about them or turning them over and over in your mind?

Yes _____ No _____

Rumination Leads You to Focus Less on the World around You

Have you ever been so involved in thinking things through in your mind that you became almost completely unaware of what was going on around you? Many people experience this periodically when they're driving a car. Other people sometimes experience it at parties or other social gatherings.

Research has shown that focusing too much attention on yourself can lead to depressed mood (Lyubomirsky and Nolen-Hoeksema 1995). How does this happen? When you're already feeling a little down and you begin to ruminate, you become less and less in touch with things outside of you. This can be a problem because things happening in your personal environment often provide important information (Pyszczynski and Greenberg 1987). For example, conversations at a party provide information about the interests of others and potential ways to meet new and interesting people. If you're turning things over and over in your mind, you can't listen to what people are saying; you might hear them, but your mind is definitely elsewhere.

Focusing your attention on yourself can also lead to reliving the past. Although things that have happened in your past don't physically exist in the present, you can feel as if they do if you think a great deal about them. One client had lost a child fifteen years before she entered therapy. She had been depressed the entire time since her daughter had passed away. As she told the story of her daughter's death, she said she felt exactly the way she had felt fifteen years ago. As she put it, "It's as if I relive it every time I think about it."

Checkpoint

Do you find that when you ruminate about problems, you are less in touch with what's happening around you?

Yes _____ No _____

People Often Believe That Rumination Is Helpful

Research has shown that many people believe that ruminating can be helpful. Those people who believe rumination can be helpful are also more likely to ruminate as a way to cope with problems (Papageorgiou and Wells 2003). This places them at risk for developing depression. You can see why believing in the value of digging deeply for your inner child could get you into trouble if you took it too far.

Exercise: What Do You Believe?

Below are several beliefs about the value of ruminating. Place a check mark next to those statements that you believe or have believed in the past.

- ☐ Thinking deeply about problems is the best way to solve them.

- ☐ You need to dig deeply to uncover your true feelings.

- ☐ You can only get rid of depression by carefully analyzing what you're feeling and why.

    □ Turning problems over and over in your mind helps you to understand them.

    □ It's better to try to solve problems after thinking about them for some time.

Do you have other beliefs about the value of rumination? What are they?

_____

_____

If you have a tendency to ruminate, you may have the sense that it's beyond your control; it's just what you do. In fact, some researchers have suggested that the tendency to think repeatedly about problems may be related to particular brain functions (Wells and Carter 2001). But your brain is only part of the picture. Simply because something about the brain is involved in a particular behavior does not mean the brain causes the behavior. In fact, the behavior may cause changes in the brain! There must be other reasons why ruminating is such a common response to depression, despite its negative effects.

Sometimes It's Helpful to Think about the Causes of Problems

There is no doubt that thinking deeply about problems can sometimes help to solve them. After all, if your car won't start, you can only fix the problem after you figure out why it's not starting. In the course of your lifetime, you have developed the ability to solve problems by analyzing them carefully. However, like any behavior, the tendency to think deeply about problems can be taken too far, or it can be used in situations where it isn't particularly helpful. Human beings are imperfect, and one of the things we all struggle with is figuring out which behaviors work in which situations. Unfortunately, ruminating often does not work well when you are feeling depressed or anxious.

Exercise: What Happens When You Ruminate?

Think about times when you ruminate, brood, worry, or in other ways turn negative things over and over in your mind. What happens while you're ruminating? How do you feel? What happens directly afterward? Do you solve problems or feel better? In the space below write down some of the consequences of this behavior.

1. _____

2. _____

3. _____

4. _____

5. _____

Ruminating as an Effective Avoidance Strategy

When you face a very difficult task or situation, worrying about it can be an effective way to avoid tackling the problem. A client named Kendra knew that she would need to find a new place to live at the first of the year. Her current roommate was getting married and the lease was about to run out. Kendra was concerned that she would not be able to find a nice place to live that was affordable or that she would end up sharing a place with someone with whom she wasn't comfortable. As it turned out, Kendra spent much more time brooding about the possibility of things not working out than she did actively looking for a new places to live. The more she became aware of this pattern, the more Kendra realized that the prospect of moving created anxiety. To solve the problem, Kendra needed to find a way to tolerate the anxiety while moving forward with her plan. Instead, she avoided moving forward, which, of course, made her depression and anxiety worse. Kendra's situation looked like this:

Topic of rumination: *Not being able to find a place to live, getting stuck with a bad roommate.*

Possible things being avoided: *Looking for a place to live, making phone calls, looking at rental listings, etc.*

Consequences of ruminating: *Feeling more depressed and worried, not making any progress on finding a place to live.*

Exercise: What Do You Ruminate About?

Is there something in your life that you've tended to ruminate about recently? Is it possible that ruminating is helping you to avoid dealing with the problem directly? In the space below, write down one thing that you have recently spent a great deal of time thinking about. Then write down one possible feeling or situation that the ruminating might be helping you to avoid. Finally, write down some consequences of the ruminating.

Topic of rumination: _____

_____

Possible things being avoided: _____

_____

Consequences of ruminating: _____

_____

PROBLEM SOLVING, EXPERIENCING, AND RUMINATING: IT'S EASY TO GET THEM CONFUSED

There is a difference between thinking about a problem in order to solve it and ruminating. When you think about a problem and you're trying to solve it, you will only think about it long enough to solve the problem, or at least to make progress on it. But when you're ruminating, you will think about problems over and over in a way that doesn't really lead anywhere, except possibly to more intense depression and anxiety.

There is also a difference between experiencing thoughts, feelings, or sensations, and ruminating about them. If something bad happens to you, such as ending a relationship, losing a job, or losing a loved one, it is quite normal to feel sad, disappointed, or even a little depressed for a while. In fact, you can run into problems if you work too hard to avoid experiencing these emotions. Yet by their nature, emotions tend to be time limited. If you allow yourself to fully experience them, they tend to pass within a few minutes, hours, days, or weeks at the longest. When you ruminate or brood over painful emotions, however, they tend to stick around much longer. Most people don't want to prolong negative thoughts or feelings, but the problem is that you can easily mistake ruminating for experiencing. In other words, you may think that you're simply experiencing your emotions when, in fact, you are ruminating about them.

HOW TO GAIN CONTROL OVER RUMINATION

Because it is so easy to get stuck in the process of ruminating, it is important to gain control over this behavior. Mulling things over in your head happens easily. Nevertheless, there are other choices you can make than to sit and ruminate.

Recognizing Rumination When It Happens

Shannon was receiving therapy for depression and had made considerable progress in activating herself. Although getting active and combating avoidance had a positive effect on her mood each day, she still found that she did not enjoy the activities as much as she had before she was depressed. During one session, Shannon reported having spent the previous Saturday playing at the park with her two young boys. Although playing with the boys was an activity that she would typically enjoy, Shannon reported feeling self-critical and unhappy about the whole experience. "What kind of mother am I that I can't even enjoy playing with my kids?" she asked.

As Shannon and her therapist looked closely at what happened, however, they realized that Shannon wasn't actually playing with her boys when she was at the park. Instead, the boys were playing on the swings while Shannon was watching from a nearby bench. Actually, Shannon wasn't even really watching the boys swing. What she was doing was thinking over and over about how much less time she spends with them since getting divorced and how awful it is for them that their parents are no longer together. The most important part of Shannon's story is that she didn't even recognize when she was ruminating. When her therapist asked her how she spent her weekend, she said, "playing with the boys at the park." But playing and ruminating are certainly different behaviors!

The first step to gaining control over rumination is to recognize when it happens. You know you're ruminating if

- You're thinking over and over about negative thoughts, feelings, or situations.

- The process of thinking over and over again is not helping you feel less depressed, more hopeful, or less self-critical.

- The process of thinking has not helped you to solve a problem.

The Two-Minute Rule for Recognizing Rumination

Once you think you might be ruminating, continue what you're doing for two minutes. Then stop and ask yourself the following three questions:

1. Have I made any progress toward solving a problem?

2. Do I understand something about a problem (or my feelings about it) that I haven't understood before?

3. Do I feel less self-critical or less depressed than before I started thinking about this?

Unless the answer to one of these questions is a clear yes, chances are you're ruminating.

RUMINATION CUES ACTION

This may seem like a strange idea, but you can actually teach yourself to use ruminating as a cue to get active. You can use the acronym RCA, which stands for "rumination cues action." A cue is something that prompts you to behave in a certain way. For example, a red stop sign is a cue to slow down an automobile and eventually stop. Unfortunately, if you tend to ruminate, then many things in your life probably cue you to do so. And, ruminating itself has probably become a cue for more ruminating. But that can change.

How RCA Can Work

A client named Peter experienced episodes of depression most of his adult life. At thirty-nine, he sometimes had the sense that he was always depressed. However, after

Exercise: Monitoring Rumination

Over the next week, see if you can recognize and label rumination when it occurs. Use the rule above to help you recognize brooding, obsessing, or other ruminating behavior. When you do recognize it, say to yourself, "This is ruminating." You will be surprised at how powerful it can be to simply increase your awareness of what you're doing. You will probably find that labeling rumination will help you to control it.

Use the space below to monitor ruminating when it happens. In the first column, record the situation in which you observed yourself ruminating. In the second column record exactly what you were ruminating about. In the third column identify the consequences of ruminating. An example of how to monitor episodes of ruminating is provided in the first row.

	Situation	Rumination	Consequence
1.	Driving to work on Monday	I'm stuck in a bad relationship. I'll never be happy or fulfilled in my life.	Felt more depressed. Almost ran a stop sign.
2.			
3.			
4.			
5.			

completing several activity monitoring charts, it became apparent that some of Peter's days were worse than others, and some times of day were particularly difficult. For example, after Peter ate dinner each night, he sat at the table thinking about what he needed to do the next day. As he thought about particular tasks, he began to think about what he had accomplished in his life and how much less it was than he had hoped. Then, Peter began to think about a long list of what he considered to be failures in his work, his family, and his love life. By the time he went to bed, Peter often felt extremely depressed.

Peter's postdinner ruminating had become a habit; it was so automatic that he was hardly aware of it. If you asked him about it, he would have said that he just starts pondering things and, before he knows it, he's engulfed in his train of thought and can't seem to stop. In therapy, Peter worked on first recognizing and labeling when he was ruminating. Then he developed a plan for responding differently to ruminating. Peter generated a list of other things he could be doing after dinner, such as reading an enjoyable book, paying bills, taking a walk, watching a movie, or calling friends or family. Peter agreed that whenever he noticed himself ruminating he would immediately get up from where he was sitting and begin one of these other activities. Rumination became a cue for action. After a week of doing this, Peter actually skipped the ruminating and went right from dinner to other activities. As a result, he often felt much less depressed when he went to bed and was able to fall asleep much more easily. When he noticed his ruminating at other times, it became a cue for action.

Over the next few days, try to put this RCA process to work. Whenever you observe yourself ruminating, label it ("This is ruminating"), and then use it as a cue to shift to a different activity. If you stick with it for a few days, you should notice a major decrease in the amount of time you spend ruminating, and your mood should improve.

YOU'RE THERE, BUT YOU'RE NOT: THE IMPORTANCE OF ATTENDING TO YOUR EXPERIENCE

Remember Shannon's story? Although she thought she was playing with her children at the park, she wasn't actually attending to the experience. Attending to an experience means paying attention both to what's going on around you and to what you are feeling, thinking, and sensing. Attending to an experience means being there psychologically rather than being somewhere else. Have you ever noticed that when you become caught up in a particular task or situation you spend much less time thinking about yourself?

The bottom line is that attending to your experience is a very powerful way to gain control over rumination. Another word for attending to experience is *mindfulness*, which is a form of meditation in daily life practiced by some Zen Buddhists. Recent research has shown that practicing mindfulness can be an effective way to combat depression (Teasdale et al. 2000). You don't have to become a Buddhist to benefit from attending to your experience, but it does take practice.

Exercise: Putting RCA to Work

Look over the list of ruminating situations you made in the table above. Now, copy each one into the column labeled "Situation" in the table below. In the next column, write down what you were ruminating about. Then, for each situation and rumination, list at least two other activities you could engage in rather than ruminating. The first row gives an example.

	Situation	Rumination	Cues	Action
1.	Driving to work on Monday	I'm stuck in a bad relationship. I'll never be happy or fulfilled in my life.	→	1. Sing along with the radio. 2. Pay attention to what I'm seeing as I drive.
2.			→	1. 2.
3.			→	1. 2.
4.			→	1. 2.
5.			→	1. 2.

Exercise: When Do You Space Out?

Below are some situations in which you may have difficulty attending to your experience. These are situations in which people sometimes space out or, if they are depressed, begin to ruminate. Place a check mark in the box next to the ones that are relevant to you.

☐ taking a walk

☐ eating a meal

☐ watching television

☐ driving in the car

☐ sitting at your desk at work

☐ being in a social setting with other people

☐ working at the computer

☐ cleaning, doing dishes

What are some other examples? _____

_____

Here are some examples of things you can attend to while taking a walk:

● sounds around you (birds, wind, cars)

● smells around you

● the feeling of walking

● sights around you (gardens, trees, plants, patterns in the sky)

Here are some examples of things you can attend to in social settings:

● what other people are saying

● the physical surroundings (are you in a house? at a park? out to dinner?)

● the taste of food or drinks

Exercise: Paying Attention

Over the next couple of days, practice attending to your experience in situations where you might normally ruminate. Below is a space for you to write down the situations you are in and the things to which you attended. We completed the first row as an example.

Day	Situation	I attended to ...
Mon.	Sitting at my desk at work	The materials I was reading, feeling my posture as I was sitting, my steady breathing

Dealing with Negative Thinking: The Power of Nonjudgmental Awareness

When we work with clients on attending to their experiences, many of them say that negative thoughts and feelings still creep into their minds at times, even when they are not ruminating. This is completely understandable. You know that you can't live your entire life without ever having negative thoughts or feelings! No one can.

It turns out that it's possible to briefly attend to the experience of negative thinking without allowing it to turn into rumination. The idea is to simply acknowledge and label negative thinking in a nonjudgmental way. Being nonjudgmental means that you are simply aware of what you are doing without judging it to be good or bad. It means to stop saying to yourself, "I've got to stop being so self-critical," or, "Oh no, here I go again with the negative thinking. Why do I always do this?" Instead, the next time you catch yourself worrying, brooding, or being self-critical, simply say to yourself, "This is negative thinking," and continue with whatever activity you're doing. The goal is to avoid getting stuck trying to get rid of the thinking or spending a lot of time dwelling on it. Simply acknowledge it and continue on. Research has shown that adopting a nonjudgmental stance toward painful thoughts and feelings can help your mood (Hayes and Gifford 1997).

CHAPTER SUMMARY

Rumination is the behavior of thinking often and deeply about what you're feeling, why you're feeling it, or what's going wrong in your life. A large amount of research has shown that the tendency to ruminate is closely associated with depressed mood. At the same time, popular media and self-help books often encourage you to look inside yourself and analyze your problems. Many people mistakenly try to cope with depression by ruminating and, in the process, make it worse by doing so. The first step to overcoming rumination is to increase your awareness of it when it happens. The second step is to substitute alternative behaviors for rumination. Some helpful alternative behaviors include allowing rumination to cue you to take action, attending to your experience ("What am I doing and experiencing right now; what's going on around me?"), and observing that you're thinking without getting caught up in what you're thinking about.

Part 3

Activation as an Approach to Your Daily Life

Chapter 6

Make Changes One
Step at a Time

When you are depressed, you may feel especially stretched to do what needs to be done. The only way to deal with the many challenges you face is to take them one small step at a time. That is the crux of this chapter, to teach you to break everything down into smaller parts.

FEELING OVERWHELMED COMES WITH THE TERRITORY

Carolyn had lost a lot of weight as a result of feeling depressed and having little to no appetite. Her first approach back into the social world was going to be a Sunday picnic with her cousins at the lake.

Carolyn knew that she needed to finish taking in her shorts, so she could go to the picnic. She had missed a great deal of work and couldn't afford to run out and get new clothes, and weather forecasts indicated that Sunday was going to be sweltering. She liked several of the shorts she owned, but they would look baggy on her now. She just needed to take an hour or two to take them in at the waist. Still, the task seemed overwhelming. "I just don't feel like getting started," she complained. "If I could only get motivated, it would be a snap."

The words "if I could only get motivated" are the cry of futility for many people who are depressed. As you have most likely experienced, depression is a reaction to life where you shut down, so to speak. When you become fatigued, you have low energy, and even the activities that you manage to engage in don't feel as pleasurable as before. Your motivation gets zapped as well.

If you had your normal amount of energy, you could get jobs done at the usual pace. However, you don't have your normal amount of energy. Depression has changed that for the time being. Just as the person with a broken jaw has to take smaller bites in order to chew without choking, you need to adjust the amount of work that you take on at any given time. Unfortunately, though, the requirements of life don't get reduced just because you are depressed. You can easily get stuck in feeling completely overwhelmed by the daily tasks of living.

Exercise: Discover What You Can Do When You're Not Depressed

Write down the activities or tasks that seem to come easily when you are not depressed, but that you seem to be incapable of accomplishing when you are depressed.

_____

_____

_____

_____

_____

_____

What do you notice about your list? Do you have little trouble accomplishing things when you're feeling depressed? Or are there several tasks with which you seem to struggle?

HOW DEPRESSION MAKES EVERYTHING SEEM WORSE

When you feel blue, everything looks gloomy. It is difficult to have hope when you are feeling blue. Without hope, the reasons for accomplishing tasks seem to fade. When tasks loom large and trigger thoughts such as "it's not worth it," the world will look even gloomier. Again, the depression loop occurs. Why does everything seem worse when you are depressed? That question is difficult to answer, but we'll venture an explanation.

Shutting Down and Shutting Out Stimulation

Symptoms that we now consider part of depression may have served human beings well at one time in the evolutionary past. Although these theories are still under investigation, they all suggest that low mood and depression have served human beings in acting as a defense against certain aversive or emotionally painful life situations. For example, Nesse (2000) has theorized that negative thinking and lack of motivation are adaptive responses that help signal that your behavior is not adaptive given the current environment. Shutting down and withdrawing helps you to stop pursuing goals that you are unlikely to achieve. These strategies can also help you stop trying to challenge dominant figures in your life, particularly in situations where to do so could bring further harm. For example, if you have an unreasonable or abusive boss, spouse, parent, or acquaintance, he or she may be a dominant figure, the loss of whom would be a greater cost than submission. In another situation, you might lose motivation in a struggle to lose weight after many years of trying and failing. In such a circumstance, the natural response is to disengage, lose interest, have decreased physical energy, or feel lethargic, and to ruminate on negative aspects of life. Does this sound similar to what you experience when you're depressed?

You become depressed for a variety of reasons. However, when depression is a reaction to life events, it may be that the reaction is one which has been with human beings for centuries. In modern life, however, the process of shutting down feels bad and puts you out of sync with your peers. Psychologists diagnose it as a disorder; similarly, the fight-or-flight response is a disorder when it functions as anxiety.

Checkpoint

Has it ever felt to you that your depression was a form of shutting down?

Yes _____ No _____

Have you ever felt that you were shutting down because it was too hard to figure out how to cope with difficult life situations?

Yes _____ No _____

When you shut down, you are less able to cope with the world around you. Life can be overstimulating. It is similar to being exhausted after a hard day of physical exertion. In such a state, the telephone ringing, a knock on the door, or horns blowing from the street, seem like further drains on your energy. It is just too hard to get up to answer the phone when your legs are so tired that they feel like Jell-O and you can barely keep your eyes open.

Sometimes Life Is Simply Overwhelming

Depression is not just about your reaction, however. You do not need to feel shut down in order for life to be overstimulating. There are some life situations that would overwhelm almost anyone. The loss of a job and the subsequent financial stresses that occur have an impact on most people; very few people can rise above the situation without a care. If you compound such a stressor with other current problems, along with issues you may have as a result of your childhood history, life can indeed be overwhelming. You can think of this as *stress exhaustion*. Too many things happening at once or one major life event that exceeds your ability to cope can cause you to become paralyzed. You then retreat, may get into frequent TRAPs, and lose motivation to put effort into activities.

This exercise may have shown you that in the past, when you were not depressed, you coped very well. Later in this chapter, the exercises will focus on getting you back into the swing of your old coping patterns. If the exercise showed you that you're now facing challenges that exceed anything you've had to deal with before, this chapter will help you to take on the challenges, one small step at a time.

SO MANY JOBS, SO LITTLE TIME

If you live in the city, getting home from work often requires a slow drive on crowded freeways or rides in crowded subways or buses. If you live in the country, getting home from work may take you a long time because you live miles away from where you are employed. Work stress, pressures from bosses, bills to pay, getting children to school and after-school activities, and fulfilling other social obligations, like church committees or a political group membership, all require time and attention. Add to that you are feeling depressed and not at your best. The point is, feeling overwhelmed by the usual jobs of life is not a fault or a personal weakness. It is understandable given the world in which we live, and the combination of environmental pressures and depression.

Kathleen was a sixty-seven-year-old widow who had worked her entire life as a registered nurse until her retirement at age sixty-five. Her husband, Artie, died of a sudden heart attack the year before Kathleen's retirement. She did not need to worry about money because her husband's life insurance policy allowed her to pay their mortgage in full and have an annual stipend to assist with living expenses. She also taught a class in a certified nurse's aid program at a local community college. Kathleen had been heartbroken following Artie's sudden death. She spent money that they had saved for a trip to Europe on an extremely expensive funeral,

Exercise: Anatomy of Stress Exhaustion

1. Write down the recent life events that have made you feel overwhelmed.

_____

_____

_____

_____

2. How have you coped with similar things in the past, when you were not depressed?

_____

_____

_____

_____

3. If you have not coped with events of this magnitude in the past, what troubles you most about the current events?

_____

_____

_____

_____

coffin, and headstone for Artie. She paid for airline tickets for his two sisters to fly across country to the funeral. She told her friends, "That money was for the two of us to enjoy a vacation. I would not enjoy going on a vacation without him." She kept the rest of the money they had saved in a savings account. She did not use any of the money for her personal enjoyment, nor did she plan to take a trip abroad.

Kathleen's mother was still living when Artie died and had just turned ninety-one. Kathleen saw her mother three times a week for a visit and to check her blood pressure. She also made trips to the pharmacy to buy her mother's medications. She found that she had greater difficulty spending time with her mother after Artie died. She kept thinking about how long her mother had lived and how young Artie was when he died. Not that she wished her mother would die, but she simply wished Artie were still alive. When her mother succumbed to a bout of pneumonia, Kathleen felt both sadness and extreme remorse.

When Kathleen entered therapy, a full year and a half after her mother's death, her grieving and loneliness had turned to an episode of clinical depression. She started therapy in November and was having such a difficult time getting things accomplished around her house that she was considering quitting her teaching job. Over time, she had become unable to take care of the basics, such as cooking and keeping house, without great difficulty. Kathleen's story provides an example of how the normal tasks of living can feel overwhelming after times of great stress or during a period of depression.

Checkpoint

Have you found that most of the things you need to do feel much bigger when you are depressed than when you are not?

Yes _____   No _____

INTERPERSONAL DYNAMICS AND THE DIFFICULTY OF RELATIONSHIPS

Some theorists believe that depression is nearly always related to problems in interpersonal relationships (Klerman et al. 1984). The chances are that interpersonal issues have either contributed to you feeling depressed, or they are affected by the fact that you are feeling depressed. Maintaining relationships takes time and energy, and relationships are often complicated in both positive and negative ways.

Consider Terry, a twenty-seven-year-old disc jockey who has had frequent bouts of depression since her late teens. Terry is mostly gregarious and has a large group of friends and acquaintances. When she is not depressed, she attends parties and meets friends for coffee and dinner. During periods of depression, however, Terry retreats from the world. Many of her acquaintances stop inviting her to social events after repeatedly getting no response from her. She has three close friends who understand her pattern and tolerate her withdrawing for months at a time, but even these relationships are somewhat strained. The loss of friendships prolongs Terry's depression, which keeps her out of touch for even longer periods of time. This is Terry's depression loop, and the interpersonal turmoil that results is a main focus of her treatment.

Exercise: Who Are the People Who Help to Sustain You?

Write down the names of those people in your past or present who have been supportive in your life:

_____

_____

_____

_____

_____

Next to the name of each person still living, write down the last time you had contact with them. Also, write down a number on a scale of 1 to 5 next to each name to rate how satisfying or enjoyable the relationship is right now. A 1 would be "not at all satisfying" and a 5 would be "extremely satisfying."

What did you notice? Are you seeing supportive people in your life on a regular basis? How satisfying or enjoyable are the relationships? If they are not satisfying or enjoyable, is it because something is wrong in the relationship? Or is it because you have been withdrawing and not spending as much quality time with them?

Now write the names of people that you know only minimally as acquaintances or coworkers:

_____

_____

_____

_____

_____

Next to each of those names, write down the last time you had contact with them. What do you see? Do you have more contact with those people who have been supportive in your life or with casual acquaintances? Put a check mark by the names of those casual acquaintances who have potential to be closer friends.

Interpersonal relationships can bring great joy or weigh negatively on a person's life. If you have supportive friends and family, you may thrive in their company. If you have relationship problems with a significant other or have come from a difficult home environment, you may feel the burden of relationships. In any case, dealing with a difficult interpersonal situation can be challenging. Confronting others is particularly difficult when you are depressed. If the difficult relationship precipitated your depression, as it does in many marital relationships (Jacobson et al. 1991), you may be loath to deal with the person. Nevertheless, you must deal with your interpersonal relationships if they are at the heart of difficulties in your life. We'll show you how to break even this vague area of relationships into steps to improve your life.

You may be wondering, how can you maintain supportive relationships when you feel gloomy all the time and don't want to be a burden on others? This is a common dilemma for people who are depressed. And it's all the more reason to use the outside-in approach and to take small steps toward maintaining your relationships. It can require some effort on your part, but there are ways to break the process down so that you don't feel overburdened.

TO GET THE JOB DONE, WRITE A JOB DESCRIPTION

You wouldn't show up for work on your first day at a new job and expect to know how to do every required task. Many employers put job descriptions in writing, to make their expectations clear. How can you expect yourself to accomplish things when you're depressed if you aren't clear on exactly what you want to accomplish and what steps are involved? Again, it is understandable that things feel difficult and overwhelming when you're depressed. We now turn our focus to how to tackle tasks that seem overwhelming, regardless of how you feel. Taking the outside-in approach is a useful method for getting started.

EVERY ACTIVITY OR CHALLENGE HAS ITS COMPONENT PARTS

It can be very helpful to break tasks and challenges down into their component parts. Although it is true in some respects that "the whole is greater than the sum of its parts," paying close attention to the parts is often necessary to find your way to the bigger picture. In behavioral psychology, this is referred to as creating a *task analysis*. For now, the important point is this: It is much easier to accomplish tasks and challenges in your life if you break them down into manageable steps. And by steps, we mean baby steps.

Any task or challenge in your life can be subjected to a task analysis. Below are a few different areas where breaking things down into steps can help you achieve your goals and bring you that much closer to ending depression.

Making and Maintaining Friends

If you feel lonely when you are depressed, or you think it would help to spend more time with people you might enjoy, you may benefit from spending more time with friends or family or by meeting some new people. Earlier you did an exercise that asked you to write down the names of casual acquaintances and to note those people who may have potential to be closer friends. If you chose one or two of those people and asked them out for coffee or to join you at a movie (a social connection that requires little sustained conversation and can be a good icebreaker), you might begin to develop some new friendships. So what steps are involved in making and maintaining friends? They might include

- making a list of people you'd like to spend more time with

- choosing a couple of people to call or write to

- having a cup of coffee or a drink with one person

- inviting friends or family over for a meal

In order to break down any interaction into parts, it helps to start from the end goal and work backward. For example, if your goal is to invite an attractive person out to dinner, the final successful step would be asking the person to join you for a night out. Notice that the final goal is *not* going out to dinner. When dealing with interpersonal interactions, setting a goal that is dependent on the other person responding in a favorable way is a setup for feeling that you have failed. Instead, set a goal that depends only on your own behavior.

Task Analysis: Asking a Person to Dinner

Once you have set your goal, you can either work backward to clarify the steps to reach it, or you can simply list everything that is necessary to accomplish the plan. The latter may be less confusing, so it's the method used in the following example.

Say your goal is to ask a person named Denise to join you for dinner. In order to ask Denise out to dinner, you must accomplish the following steps:

1. Plan that you will see Denise in order to provide an opportunity to ask her for dinner. (If you already have her telephone number or e-mail address, you can contact her by phone or e-mail.)

2. Choose several possible evenings for dinner so that you and Denise can compare schedules and arrange a time that is convenient for you both.

3. Write down the possible times so that you can remember them if you feel nervous about extending the invitation.

4. If you feel nervous about how to ask, you can write a script for yourself to memorize.

   - The script should include telling Denise that you would enjoy sharing dinner.

   - The script should also include suggestions for the date of the dinner.

- The script should include suggestions for the time of the dinner.

- The script should include suggestions for the restaurant.

- The script may also include alternatives if she is not available for dinner, such as meeting for coffee.

5. If you are asking in person, make good eye contact, but don't stare without looking away naturally.

6. If you are writing an e-mail, check your spelling before sending it off.

7. If calling on the telephone, first ask her if it is a good time to talk. You might say, "Did I catch you at an okay time?"

This list is not meant to be comprehensive or to represent every social interaction in which you might find yourself. It is an example of some of the components involved in an apparently easy task of asking someone out to dinner. Now that you have seen a brief example, you might want to try this yourself by breaking down an interaction that has already occurred.

Having a Difficult Conversation

Conflict can occur in any relationship. Avoiding conflict that needs to be resolved will only keep you feeling depressed and shut down. On the other hand, verbally attacking people out of anger is unlikely to be helpful either. Also, confronting some people may result in very negative consequences for you, such as getting reprimanded at work or fired from your job. For all of these reasons, it is better to approach people with a good plan in mind.

Now think about a current challenge. Asking someone to dinner, as in the example above, may not be difficult for you. It may be more difficult to share personal information about yourself with someone to whom you wish to get closer. Or perhaps, you need to confront someone who is important in your life.

Task Analysis: Sharing Hurt Feelings

Consider the example of telling your partner or spouse that he or she hurt your feelings by staying out very late after work and not calling to tell you. In this situation it would be important to keep in mind that the goal is expressing your feelings, not eliciting an apology or promise for change in your partner's behavior. Although the latter may be a desirable outcome, you cannot count on it, so you would set your goal to be within your control. Here are some steps:

1. Decide the specific behavior of your partner that hurt your feelings and plan to express your feeling about that. In this example, feelings were hurt because your partner did not call to tell you that he or she was going to be out late after work. You have no problem with your spouse going out after work, but you want to be called. Or, if the

Exercise: Breaking Down the Components of an Interpersonal Interaction

Step 1: Think of a recent interaction that was difficult for you but that you believe you successfully negotiated. This could have been a tense encounter with a lover or spouse, an interaction with your boss, or any other difficult interaction with another person or group of people. Try to think of the encounter in as much detail as you can remember.

Step 2: Write down all of the steps of the interaction. That is, what were all of the things you needed to do to engage in this interaction successfully? (If you need more space, continue on a separate sheet of paper.)

1. _____

_____

2. _____

_____

3. _____

_____

4. _____

_____

5. _____

_____

6. _____

_____

7. _____

_____

8. _____

_____

9. _____

_____

10. _____

_____

issue was that you didn't know your partner's whereabouts, which caused you to worry, then express that concern. Keep it simple, so you can stay on track.

2. Plan an appropriate time to speak with your partner and make either a mental or written note for yourself.

3. It may help to rehearse what you plan to say to your partner. Again, the simplest statement is the best. Something like, "I know you had a good time with your friends last week, and I'm happy that you enjoyed yourself. However, when you didn't call me, I was worried and felt hurt that you didn't let me know you'd be late so that I could rest assured that you were all right." (If you feel more confident with a script, write it down and try to commit it to memory.)

4. When both you and your partner are at home, tell him or her that you would like to talk at the specific time.

5. Ask if that time is convenient for your partner.

6. At the appointed time invite your partner to sit with you in a location that is comfortable for the two of you.

7. Tell your partner what you planned to say.

All of this looks very formal and strict. In reality it might look like this:

You: Hi, can we take a few minutes tonight at eight, before the good shows are on, so I can talk to you? Is that a good time for us to talk?

Partner: Is something wrong?

You: No, nothing serious, but I'd just like a few minutes of your time.

Partner: How about now?

You: (*sticking to the plan*) Well, let's make it eight o'clock, if that's okay, so that we can eat dinner first.

Partner: Okay.

At eight o'clock, the conversation could go like this:

You: I know you had a good time with your friends last week, and I'm happy that you enjoyed yourself. However, when you didn't call me, I was worried and felt hurt that you didn't let me know you'd be late so that I could rest assured that you were all right.

Partner: Is that what you wanted to talk about?

You: Yes, that's all, but it's important to me.

Partner: I realize it was thoughtless, but I really didn't think you'd worry. I didn't intend to hurt your feelings. I'll remember to call before doing that again.

You: Thanks, I'd appreciate that.

Should your partner not have responded well, you would still have achieved your main goal: to express a hurt. The conversation could even go on further, and still be productive, even if your partner responds poorly. Let's assume that your partner said something like, "I don't need to tell you where I am every minute of the day. You aren't my parent!" Instead of responding with, "See, selfish, you don't care about me at all," you would stick to your goal by saying, "I realize that you aren't obliged to get my permission, and that's not what I'm asking for. My feelings were hurt that you didn't call and I was left at home worrying. That's all."

Types of Human Interactions

Human interactions are not just about conversing or confronting. There are many ways to interact with others. Below is a list of possibilities. You can

1. Be physically around other people.

2. Interact through telephone calls or e-mails.

3. Have brief interactions at grocery stores, waiting for the bus, at coffee shops, etc.

4. Make eye contact to acknowledge another person.

5. Give a verbal or symbolic greeting (such as a nod of the head or a handshake).

6. Notice characteristics of the other person (such as eye color, what he or she is wearing).

7. Offer a token ("I'm going to get a cup of coffee, would you like something?").

8. Ask for a favor ("Could you reach that bottle of cleanser for me? The shelf is too high.").

9. Share what you have in common ("What a cute little dog! Mine is exactly like that.")

10. Make small talk such as mentioning the weather ("Great day for this time of year"); referring to a sports event ("How about those Mariners?"); inquiring about family ("Is your brother well?"); mentioning a recent event in your life ("I just came back from a weekend at the beach"); asking about a recent event in the other person's life ("Did you do anything enjoyable over the weekend?").

When you are depressed, you may think that small talk is stupid or irrelevant. It is, as the words suggest, conversation about small things. Consider it social axle grease. Small talk helps ease you into a conversation or social exchange. You may also think that because you are depressed you have little to offer or nothing good to say. It would be a turnoff to others if you recited a list of everything that troubles you whenever they encounter you. However, you can create a positive interaction by asking others about themselves or by simply saying, "I didn't do very much this weekend," or "I've been a little under the weather," if you prefer not to imply that everything is fine. But making the effort to interact with others keeps you from falling into an avoidance pattern that could ultimately leave you feeling more isolated and depressed.

Cleaning the House

Human interactions are a basic part of life. However, there are other basic functions that can seem overwhelming when you are depressed. A frequent difficulty for many people is keeping up with housecleaning.

Checkpoint

When you feel depressed, do you leave basic chores undone and feel worse because your home is a mess and you feel that it is difficult to keep up?

Yes _____ No _____

When even the little tasks in life are overwhelming, every day can bring a feeling of failure. When you awaken to confront a countertop cluttered with dirty dishes or a pile of undone laundry, you are in a setup for a TRAP. The mess and clutter is the trigger, the response is either to feel disgusted, blue, or fatigued, and the avoidance pattern is to escape in some way. Alternative coping would be to get the job done. When you think, "I've got to clean up this place," however, the task can be daunting. This is why breaking tasks down into manageable parts can be helpful. Let's take the example of cleaning a closet that is filled with shoes, old hangers, sweaters lying on the floor and tossed on a shelf, and old clothes that you can no longer wear. What are the steps?

1. Clear an area outside the closet to have room to sort things.

2. Get some bags to put old clothes in for donation to a charity or for tossing in the garbage.

3. Start by picking up old hangers and placing them in a pile or tying them together to either return to the cleaners or toss in the trash.

4. Search through the pile of clothes for those that are torn and ready to throw away.

5. Look again through the pile of clothes for those that you can no longer wear because they don't fit properly, and place them in a separate pile for donation.

6. Make one more search through the clothes for those that you just don't want to keep any longer, and place them in the donation pile.

7. Fold the clothes in the donation pile so that they will fit in the bags.

8. Place the folded pile of clothes in bags for charity.

9. Pick up all sweaters (that did not go in the trash pile or charity pile) off the floor and place them in another pile outside of the closet.

10. Take all the sweaters off the shelf and add them to the pile.

11. Fold all the sweaters neatly.

12. If the shelf is too high to reach, get a stepping stool or chair and arrange the sweaters neatly on the shelf.

13. Sort your shoes into pairs.

14. Start a pile for any shoes that you wish to donate.

15. Start a second pile for shoes you wish to throw away.

16. Place the pairs of shoes you are donating in a bag.

17. Take the pairs of shoes that you are keeping and place them neatly on a shelf, in a section of the closet floor, or in a shoe rack (whichever you prefer).

18. Take the bags of clothing and shoes for donation and place them by your front door.

19. Throw the trash into the garbage.

Wow, nineteen steps! If you are thinking, "This is making me more anxious and depressed than I was before," keep the following in mind: When completing a task like cleaning your closet, the point is to tackle one step at a time. When you start a step, try not to think about the next step(s) until you are finished with the one you're doing. Then, you can make a decision about whether to continue on with another step.

Applying for a Job

For many people, applying for a job means facing the very situation that may have contributed to their depression in the first place. Being unemployed is scary and humiliating. In a tough economy, when jobs are scarce, job searches are disheartening.

This book is not intended to be a how-to on getting a job or housekeeping. However, doing a task that is daunting when you are depressed sometimes requires a little kick start. Here are a few basic components to finding a job:

- Make a list of all previous jobs and the dates you held them.

- Or update your resume. There are several free Web sites that help you to write a resume; a simple Internet search can lead you to them. Thus searching the Internet would become your first step.

- Get copies of local newspapers to read help-wanted advertisements.

- Do an online search for positions available in your field or location.

- Call an employment agency to register for their services.

- Register with a temporary agency.

- Contact potential employers through the medium they suggest (sending a resume or application over the Internet, mailing a letter of interest, telephoning for an appointment, going for a face-to-face interview). Note that each of these steps can be further broken down into smaller components.

- Go for interviews when available.

Job searches provide the potential for many TRAPs and are frustrating even for people who tend to be optimistic. They can be even more frustrating when you are depressed. Breaking tasks down into component parts helps to create reasonable bites to take on larger projects, but it does not help with the emotional component of it all. The next chapter deals entirely with ways to continue pursuing goals when you don't feel like it.

COMPLETING TASKS IN HIERARCHICAL STEPS

Joseph Wolpe and Arnold Lazarus (1966), two leaders in the field of behavior therapy, developed a method for measuring how much distress different activities create for different people. Although this technique was developed for treatment of anxiety and phobias, it is also useful when you are depressed because it provides help in facing things that you are generally avoiding. The technique is called the subjective units of discomfort scale, or SUDS. The idea is that you rate your level of discomfort based on how you feel, not based on an outside scale of distress. In other words, the scale is based on what you feel in particular situations, not on what others might feel, or on what you think you *should* feel. Your discomfort is rated from 0 to 100 in units of 10. Situations or parts of a task that cause you no discomfort or distress would be rated 0, and the most distressing events would be rated 100. Using the scale from 0 to 100 with a task analysis can help to face challenging emotional situations. Here's how it works.

Creating a SUDS Rating Scale

Since SUDS is a subjective measure, you must create your own scale of discomfort, based on your experience. How you define discomfort will vary, depending on the task you are going to approach. Different tasks may make you feel frustrated, sad, scared, discouraged, angry, or tired. To create a SUDS scale, you would have to think about each step within that task and assign that step a number reflecting the degree of stress you feel about taking that step. Since SUDS was first developed for phobias, let's look at an example of someone trying to face a fear of dogs. Notice how different interactions with dogs cause higher or lower levels of discomfort for the person who is phobic:

Scale	Experience
100	*Having my face licked by a large dog like a Newfoundland*
90	*Petting a large dog when it is not facing me and when it is being held by its owner*
80	*Seeing a large dog playing with its owner across a fence from me*
70	*Having my face licked by a small dog like a toy poodle*
60	*Petting a small dog when it is not facing me and when it is being held by its owner*
50	*Seeing a small dog playing with its owner across a fence from me*
40	*Having my face licked by a puppy*
30	*Petting a puppy when it is not facing me and is being held by its owner*
20	*Seeing a puppy playing with its owner across a fence from me*
10	*Seeing a puppy at a distance of about one city block*
0	*Seeing a photograph of a dog or puppy*

This person's ultimate goal was to allow a large, friendly dog to lick his face. Using this scale, he was able to see that other interactions with dogs would be less distressful. To reach the ultimate goal, he could start with the easiest interaction (looking at a photograph of a dog) and gradually increase the difficulty of the interactions.

Creating a SUDS scale can help you accomplish tasks too. Imagine that the task of going through the belongings of a deceased loved one will cause you a great deal of sadness along the way. Using a SUDS scale for this task, you could rate different steps from 0 to 100, where 0 means the step will cause you no sadness and 100 means the step will cause you the most sadness. Your list of steps might look like this:

- Going into his or her room: 10

- Sorting through old pictures and deciding which ones to keep: 90

- Going through old clothes and putting those to be donated into a pile: 60

- Throwing away unnecessary old papers and other personal documents: 20

In this way, you can measure the relative difficulty of different steps in a given task. Just think of what components are involved and rate each one. Once you have rated the steps, you can choose to do a task by starting with easier steps first.

This method is called a *graded task assignment*. You are starting with the easier steps and then moving upward. The goal is to face something that you'd rather avoid, but you do it in a graded fashion rather than by just jumping in.

Exercise: Completing a Task Using SUDS

Please photocopy this exercise for future use. You can use this exercise to complete any task that you are having difficulty doing.

1. Think of a task that you need to do.

   What is it? _____

2. Define the emotion that you are most likely to feel when you make an attempt to activate and complete this task that you've been avoiding.

   Main emotion experienced when attempting this task: _____

3. List the components (or steps) of this task, and rate the emotional intensity of each component based on how you have felt or believe you would feel completing each component of this task. Use the SUDS scale of 0 to 100 to describe the measure of intensity for each component. Remember, 0 means no discomfort and 100 means maximum discomfort.

Task Components   SUDS Rating

1. _____   _____

2. _____   _____

3. _____   _____

4. _____   _____

5. _____   _____

6. _____   _____

7. _____   _____

8. _____   _____

9. _____   _____

10. _____   _____

11. _____   _____

12. _____   _____

13. _____   _____

14. _____   _____

15. _____   _____

4. Begin with a component that causes mild distress and complete that component.

5. Gradually increase the difficulty of the components (step-by-step) until you complete the task.

To complete any task, it is often best to begin with those steps that cause you the least discomfort. This will help you to have successful experiences and to increase your confidence that you can tackle the next step. But remember, keep your eye on the ball. Only tackle one step at a time, and when you're done, consciously choose whether you want to tackle the next step or take a break.

Exercise: Reviewing the Process When the Task Is Done

Once you've completed an entire task, it is time to evaluate and assess the process. In the space below, write down your impressions of the entire process, including what you learned, how you feel about it now that it's over, what you've accomplished, and anything else that seems important.

_____

_____

_____

_____

_____

SUCCESS THROUGH SMALL STEPS

Martha lived in a studio apartment in a building surrounded by evergreen trees. She also lived in a city that was notoriously dark through much of the year. Her apartment faced north with the exception of a small window over the kitchen sink. She had been depressed for over six months. During that time her apartment had become cluttered and dirty. The apartment building was near a construction site where there was a great deal of dust and dirt that covered the windows. Martha's window over the sink was also near her stovetop, and she had burned several things during her depression when she went to lie down while cooking and forgot to turn the burner off.

Martha did a graded task assignment of cleaning her sink, stove, and countertops. She included the windowsill over the sink as part of the task. As she worked her way through the task, step-by-step, she discovered that cleanup did not take as long as she feared. With scheduled breaks, the entire task took her one full Saturday.

When Martha washed the windowsill over the sink, her sponge touched the window itself. There was a clear streak contrasting that little spot with the grayish film that covered the window. Although it wasn't an assigned task, Martha washed the entire glass of the window over her sink. She felt better when her sink, stove, and countertops were clean. She was not sure if she was less depressed, but at least she had made steps toward a cleaner apartment. The next morning, however, when she woke to the sunrise shining through the only eastern facing window in her apartment, she was amazed at the amount of light, even on this autumn morning. She had a greater feeling of well-being that morning.

Getting It Right

Jenna worked for her mother-in-law in a florist shop. They had a good relationship, and Jenna thought that she was paid well enough. However, Jenna needed to change her schedule because she wanted to take a class at the local community college. A change in Jenna's schedule would require her mother-in-law to switch hours with Jenna. Furthermore, Jenna's mother-in-law hoped that Jenna would continue in the florist business and always got nervous when Jenna explored other career options. Jenna didn't like asking for special consideration. During this time period when she was depressed, it was doubly difficult. However, Jenna wanted to explore getting into nursing school; she thought that it would be a more meaningful career for her. She needed to talk with her mother-in-law.

She set as her goal to ask her mother-in-law on Monday and outlined these steps:

1. Have two possibilities for changing her schedule to give her mother-in-law options.

2. Choose a time when it was usually quiet in the shop and the two women could have coffee together.

3. Script her request.

4. Memorize the script.

5. Buy two cups of coffee

6. Make the request.

When she made the request, her mother-in-law did not answer at first. Instead she asked irrelevant questions, such as, "What if you have kids? Wouldn't this be a great place to work?" Jenna kept to the topic and continued to gently ask for an answer.

Mother-in-law: Nursing school is a big commitment. Are you sure you want to start down that path?

Jenna: I know it is a big commitment, but I need to change my hours so that I can take a class and see how I do.

Mother-in-law: I thought you and Bobby were thinking of having a family. How will you do that with a nurse's schedule? Isn't it easier here?

Jenna: Yes, it is easier here. The hours are flexible, which is why I'd like to take this opportunity to take a few classes. Do either of the changes work for you?

Mother-in-law: Well, I would need to change my bridge group time.

Jenna: Well, I gave you two options. Do both require you to do that?

Mother-in-law: No, but the other option doesn't work at all. I'm not going to open the shop on Monday mornings. I did that for too many years. I've been really happy having you here to do that. It has been enormously helpful. I don't want to change that.

Jenna: Well, do the women in your bridge club have flexible schedules?

Mother-in-law: Sheila owns her business and makes her hours. Mary and Carmen don't work outside of the house.

Jenna: Then they might be able to shift around, but I only have two options for taking this class. I really would like you to consider the change.

Mother-in-law: Well, I think it is a lot of time for something that may turn out to be completely impractical. But if you want to do it, I think I can change my schedule for bridge. I'll call the others this evening and see what they can do. Is it alright if I get back to you tomorrow?

Jenna: I don't have to register until next Tuesday, so you have plenty of time to work it out on your end. Thanks.

CHAPTER SUMMARY

Using graded task assignments and task analyses to break down larger challenges can serve as an alternative coping strategy for many of the TRAPs that you encounter. This method can help you to make the overwhelming things doable. Begin by rating the discomfort you would feel with various components of a task. Then tackle each component one step at a time. Finally, consider the outcomes of the task. What effect did it have on your mood? How satisfied are you with the outcome?

Chapter 7

Free Yourself from Mood Dependence

This chapter is about freeing yourself from dependence on your moods. Your moods are different collections of feelings that you experience. When you're in a depressed mood, you may feel any combination of sadness, guilt, hopelessness, pessimism, anger, and so on. Being dependent on your mood means letting your mood dictate how you will behave and what goals you will pursue. When your behavior is mood dependent, you may find yourself saying things like, "How can I possibly work on anything right now when I have no motivation at all?" or "I couldn't possibly socialize with friends or family right now because I'm too depressed." Instead, you wait to engage in these behaviors until you have more motivation, or until you feel less depressed. An alternative is to begin and continue pursuing particular goals or activities, regardless of what mood you're in. This is a very powerful skill that takes a bit of practice. This chapter will walk you through the necessary steps to achieve goals, no matter how you feel in the moment.

THE POWER OF MOOD DEPENDENCE

Danielle was a high school history teacher in a large city. One of the reasons she decided to become a teacher was so she could enjoy the downtime during the summer months. However, over the last couple of years, she had begun to notice a certain level of depression creeping into her summer vacation. Although she continued to do things that she enjoyed, such as taking walks on the beach and getting together with friends, she did them less often. Instead, Danielle spent more time at home worrying about the coming school year and feeling guilty for not putting more time into developing her lesson plans. Despite the guilt and worry, she left most of the work for the last few weeks before school started. On some level, Danielle recognized that all the worrying and feeling guilty didn't help her to get more accomplished. However, she just couldn't seem to bring herself to start working. In her words, "I just feel way too depressed to make any headway on this stuff."

Waiting for her mood or her motivation to improve played a big part in keeping Danielle stuck. The less active Danielle was, the worse she felt, and the worse she felt, the harder it was to become active and engaged in her life. Something had to change. One morning toward the end of the summer, Danielle woke up feeling very anxious about the start of the school year and guilty about not having started her preparations sooner. Her first impulse was to lie in bed and read a book. However, on this particular morning, she said to herself, "I can't do this anymore. No matter how awful I feel, I've got to get up and do something." Danielle ate a quick breakfast and took off for the beach feeling anxious and guilty the whole way there. Surprisingly, once she was at the beach and taking a walk, Danielle noticed that her mood improved a great deal. She barely felt guilty or anxious at all. Once she observed the shift in her mood, Danielle realized something important: if she had waited for the anxiety and guilt to go away before taking action, she never would have made it to the beach. And, in all likelihood, her mood would not have improved.

Checkpoint

Can you relate to Danielle's story?

Yes _____ No _____

Have you ever found yourself thinking that there was just no way you could get going on a project because of how depressed you felt?

Yes _____ No _____

Danielle's tendency to let her moods guide her behavior is not unusual. Many people behave according to how they feel at a particular point in time. Mood-dependent behavior is behavior that is guided by how you feel in the moment, rather than by the goals you want to accomplish. For example, you may have the goal of making several repairs to your home. At any particular point in time, you may not feel like doing the work because your mood is too depressed. If you choose to avoid doing the work, your behavior is being guided by your mood rather than your goal.

Exercise: Do You Tend to Be Mood Dependent?

This tendency to rely on your mood for guidance can become a real problem when you're depressed. After all, when you're depressed, your mood is telling you not to do anything! Below are some examples of mood-dependent behavior. Put a check mark next to behaviors that describe what you do.

- ☐ Waiting until you feel less depressed to begin a chore

- ☐ Lying in bed or on the couch when you feel fatigued, rather than getting active

- ☐ Avoiding making commitments or plans with others because you're not sure how you'll feel at the time

- ☐ Canceling plans or activities at the last minute because you don't feel up to it

What are some other behaviors of yours that could be mood dependent?

_____

_____

_____

_____

Do You Assume That Your Behavior Must Follow Your Mood?

You may make the assumption, without even realizing it, that your behavior must be guided by your mood. In Western cultures, you are taught that emotions and moods are the causes of behaviors. The idea is so common that it can be hard to imagine otherwise. If you ask why a person is crying, the most common answer is, "because they're sad." If you ask why someone is smiling, you are told it's "because they're happy." People frown because they're angry, sleep too much because they're depressed, and so on.

Psychologists have learned over the last several decades that moods and emotions are actually only one of the factors that affect how people behave. Other factors include the situation you are in, what you are thinking, and what particular goals and expectations you may have in mind. Therefore, it is certainly not the case in all situations that you must act according to how you feel.

A Thought Experiment

Imagine that some friends have invited you out to dinner on a Saturday night and you agree to join them. As evening approaches, however, you feel fatigued and begin to worry that you will not enjoy yourself at dinner. You're also concerned that your friends will not enjoy your company and will wish they had not invited you. The more you think about these things, the worse you feel and the harder it is to imagine yourself making it to dinner. You decide to call and cancel.

Now imagine that someone was willing to pay you $500 to go to dinner with your friends. Would you go, even though your mood told you not to? What about for $1,000, for $300, or for $50? This may seem silly, but it raises a very important point: It is almost always possible to act independently of your mood if you choose to do so.

When you're depressed, you will tend to lose sight of this fact. You're likely to think, "I can't possibly go to dinner with friends. I feel so depressed." When you say such things to yourself often enough, you begin to believe them. If you act on that belief, the belief becomes a self-fulfilling prophecy. You forget that you are actually capable of doing almost anything, no matter how depressed your mood is. Every once in a while, you may be reminded that you don't have to be ruled by your moods. At times in the past, you may have forced yourself to do something potentially enjoyable even though you weren't in the right mood at first, and then found that you actually enjoyed yourself. Not that it's easy to do things when you're depressed; indeed, it can be extremely challenging at times. However, if you've made it this far in the workbook, you know that self-activation, although not always easy, is a powerful way to work on ending depression.

Checkpoint

Do you tend to let your behavior be guided by your mood when you're depressed?

Yes _____   No _____

Do you tend to assume that your behavior must follow your mood?

Yes _____   No _____

But Isn't It True That Emotions and Moods Influence Behavior?

You may be wondering how we could argue that emotions and moods could have so little power over behavior. After all, doesn't it seem obvious that the way you feel has a powerful effect on what you do? If you do have these questions, the following couple of sections cover some basic information about moods and emotions and further develop the idea of breaking free from mood dependence. If you feel comfortable with the idea that behavior isn't necessarily dependent on your mood, you may want to skip ahead.

Exercise: What Do You Think Is Stopping You?

Think of an activity that you have recently avoided, but that you suspect would be helpful to you in the long run. Some examples might include getting a resume together, beginning to exercise regularly, seeing friends or family more often, or confronting a difficult situation at work or at home. In the space below, write the activity or behavior that might be helpful in the long run but that you've been avoiding:

_____

_____

_____

Now consider what keeps you from engaging in this activity or behavior. Fill in the blanks below with explanations you typically give yourself. You can't engage in this activity or behavior because

1. _____

2. _____

3. _____

4. _____

5. _____

6. _____

Take a look at the reasons you listed. How many of them refer to your mood or your feelings? How many of them refer to thoughts or predictions about the consequences of doing the behavior? How many of them are real obstacles that actually keep you from doing the behavior? In other words, how many are obstacles that would be in the way even if your mood were different? What do you notice?

What Is the Purpose of Moods and Emotions?

Emotions are a basic part of being human. All humans have a wide range of feelings about events in their lives. Emotions and moods can be helpful because they signal to you that important events are happening in your life. For example, the emotion of fear signals to you that you are in a potentially dangerous situation. Happiness signals to you that something positive has happened. As a result, you may be more likely to pursue similar situations in the future. Below are other examples of moods or emotions and what they signal.

Mood/Emotion	Signals
Anxious	Something bad might happen.
Playful	Things are lighthearted.
Calm	There's nothing to worry about; you're safe.
Irritable	Something or someone is bothering you.
Depressed	Things aren't working in your life.
Ashamed	You've broken some social norm or expectation.

Do Moods and Emotions Cause Behavior?

The answer to the question of whether emotions cause behavior is yes and no. Certainly your moods influence your behavior. For example, when you feel depressed, you are probably less likely to smile or laugh at jokes. However, the idea that your moods cause (rather than just influence) your behavior creates problems. The biggest problem is that if you think this way about your own behavior, you can come to believe it. In other words, if you go around assuming that how you feel dictates what you will do at any particular point in time, what you do will always be dependent on your mood.

The fact is that although moods can have an influence, they certainly don't strictly control your behavior. This is easy to see if you consider situations in which you had to behave in a particular way, regardless of your mood at the time.

The truth is that moods and emotions are not always reliable indicators of the most helpful behavior in a situation. Have you ever felt very anxious or afraid when there wasn't anything to be afraid of? Maybe you've avoided going to the dentist or the doctor out of fear or anxiety. Or perhaps you've avoided getting together with friends or family because your mood told you it wouldn't be enjoyable. In both of these situations, moods and emotions are guiding behaviors (avoiding the dentist or doctor, avoiding getting together with others) that aren't particularly helpful and may be harmful in the long run. The bottom line is this: Even though your moods and emotions serve many useful purposes, they can also mislead you if they cue behaviors that are not helpful.

WHAT'S THE ALTERNATIVE?

You may wonder what else other than your moods can guide your behavior. When you are depressed or anxious, it can be much more helpful to behave according to a predetermined plan or set of goals rather than according to your mood. The value of plans and goals was particularly clear in Barrett's case.

Barrett had been recently laid off from a senior position in a prominent advertising agency. Although such changes were common in his field, Barrett took it personally and experienced a big blow to his self-esteem. He knew that he needed to look for another job, but he couldn't bring himself to do it. Barrett had made many connections with other agencies and clients over the last several years, and he was reasonably confident that he could find a new position if he could just get on the phone and begin networking. The problem was that whenever he thought about picking up the phone, he felt extremely depressed. All he could focus on was the shame he would feel when telling people he was laid off.

With the help of his therapist, Barrett came up with a plan for working on finding a new job. To keep things manageable, Barrett decided to spend fifteen minutes over the next three days (from 10:00 to 10:15 each morning) phoning people that might have leads for him. The important part was that, no matter how awful he felt, Barrett would stick to his plan and continue making calls. He wrote down a commitment to pursuing this goal and signed it to help himself keep the commitment. He also wrote out a script (see chapter 6) for himself, so he would be better prepared. The first fifteen minutes felt awkward, but Barrett was surprised how much easier making calls became after he'd practiced. He also noticed that his mood improved more than a little as a result of taking this bit of action each day.

Being Proactive vs. Reacting

Barrett was learning to be proactive rather than to react to his moods. When you behave reactively, you wait to see how your mood is and then decide what to do. Behaving proactively means determining a goal and pursuing it, regardless of what your mood is like. The goal doesn't need to be a lofty one; it could be as small as opening a collection of piled-up letters or bills. Behaving proactively would involve saying something like, "When I wake up tomorrow morning, I will pour myself some coffee and then immediately begin dealing with the letters or bills." Then, no matter what your mood was like, you would stick to the plan.

Here's another way to think about behaving proactively. Imagine finding yourself lost in the mountains after several days of hiking. What would you do? You would probably do whatever you could to find your way back. For example, you might form a plan of how to find civilization (follow the river?). Or, you might try to build a fire to send an emergency smoke signal. What you most likely would not do is wait to begin dealing with your situation until your mood improved or you felt more motivated. Struggling with depression is not all that different from being lost in the mountains. When you're depressed, sticking to your plan is often much more helpful than letting your mood determine what you will do to solve the problem.

Exercise: Turning Reactive Behavior into Proactive Behavior

Under the first heading below, write down examples of your behavior that are very dependent on your mood. For example, if you often choose not to exercise because you don't feel up to it, you could write "not exercising because I'm not in the mood." For each reactive behavior, write down a corresponding proactive behavior in the right-hand column. Continuing with the previous example, you could write "exercising on Monday, Wednesday, and Friday, no matter what kind of mood I'm in."

Reactive Behavior   Proactive Behavior

1. _____   _____

   _____   _____

2. _____   _____

   _____   _____

3. _____   _____

   _____   _____

Do You Have Questions?

The idea that it's often helpful to behave according to goals rather than to moods may raise questions for you.

What about the times you're so depressed that you just can't do anything? Perhaps you've had times when you felt so depressed or sad that it felt like you couldn't do anything except sit and stare or lie in bed. The key word here is "felt." Even though it feels like you can't possibly do anything, in fact you have the ability engage in other activities. Moods such as severe depression can be very strong and can almost convince you that you have no choice in how you behave. At such times, it helps to remember that if the incentive were strong enough, you could do any number of things such as exercise, clean the house, spend time with friends or family, go for a walk, write a letter, and so on. Ending depression can be a very worthwhile goal. Reminding yourself of your ability to choose what you want to do with your time can help you keep the goal in mind.

What if sometimes you're not physically capable of pursuing your goals? There are times when illnesses and injuries make it almost impossible to pursue particular goals. If you have a sprained ankle, for example, you may have great difficulty exercising. But notice that the difficulty here is due to a physical ailment and not to mood dependence. Sometimes it's hard to tell the difference between moods and physical ailments. For example, when your mood is depressed, physical aches and pains can seem more severe than if you were not depressed. For this reason, you need to consider how much of your choice to avoid being proactive is due to actual physical problems and how much is due to the effect your mood has on how you experience the problems. You may have a cold, for example, and decide that you're too sick to follow your plan to work in the garden for two hours on Saturday. How sick are you, really? Is your mood the real issue when you're telling yourself it's your cold?

Isn't it false to act like you're not depressed when you are depressed? When you act according to your goals rather than according to your mood, it may feel awkward at first. You may feel like you're "acting," in the sense of pretending you're someone that you're not. This feeling is to be expected. It does not mean that you are being false or untruthful about who you really are. In fact, the truth is that you are someone who is pursuing a goal and choosing, regardless of your mood, to act on it. Don't fall into the trap of assuming that your moods are the best reflection of who you really are. Moods are like the weather; they always affect how you see things, but they are not necessarily the best indicator of what's true or important in a particular situation. Just like there's nothing false about taking a walk when it's raining, there's nothing false about smiling and talking to people when you're depressed.

So you're just supposed to pretend you're not depressed? This question is similar to the one above. The answer is that you don't need to pretend you're in a happy mood to break free from mood dependence. The idea is to feel what you feel and continue pursuing your goals. It's as if you're saying, "I know that I am in a depressed mood right now *and* I'm going to continue with my plan to . . ." Have you ever had a cast on your arm, or other injury that made it difficult but not impossible to drive a car or do other basic activities necessary to get through your day? In these cases, it probably never occurred to you to try to pretend that you were not injured. However, once the cast was off and you were in physical therapy, you would be encouraged to use your full range of motion and not favor the arm, even though you might feel like doing so. You would begin to use the arm as if it had not been broken in order to regain full use over time.

Defining Goals for Yourself

In chapter 6, you learned to break tasks down into component parts in order to accomplish them when you are feeling depressed. Properly identifying your goals and working toward a goal when you are depressed is so important that it warrants further discussion. One tricky thing about goals and depression is that you may feel that you have no goals, or that you just don't care, or that there's no point in defining goals because you won't achieve them. This can be regarded as mood-dependent thinking. Now that you have a good idea of how to break free from mood-dependent behavior, you can apply the same principles to the thought that you have no goals or that it isn't worth bothering. For example, if you find yourself not interested in setting goals, but you are aware that it could be helpful, why not make up and pursue some goals, regardless of how you feel or think right now? Remember, feelings and moods are not always the best indicator of what's helpful.

What Are Your Short-Term Goals?

If you're going to behave according to your goals, you need to have a clear sense of what your goals are. Try thinking of a goal as something specific that you would like to see happen in the future. Helpful goals are those that you have some influence over and are objectives that you value. It also helps to make your goals concrete. For example, if your goal is to "be happier more often," it may be difficult to measure your progress. How much more happy are you supposed to be and how often? You might be better off with the goal of cutting in half the amount of time you spend worrying or ruminating and replacing this time with other activities that you enjoy. It's much easier to evaluate your progress toward this goal. It's also possible to clearly spell out the actions necessary to achieve it.

Goals can be divided into short-term and long-term. You can think of short-term goals as things you would like to accomplish in the next few days or weeks. Long-term goals are things you would like to accomplish over longer periods of time. Justine, for example, had a long-term goal of finding a job in the entertainment industry. In the short term, her goals were to find a part-time job that would allow her some free time and to fix up her house so she could sell it if she had to move. Justine could have broken down the short-term goals even further to specify the steps she needed to take to accomplish these two goals.

Exercise: Finding Your Goals

In the space below, write down as many goals as you can think of. Don't worry at this point whether they are short- or long-term goals, whether you are capable of achieving them, how hard they will be, or anything else that distracts you from your current goal, which is to think of as many goals as you can! What are your goals?

1. _____

2. _____

3. _____

4. _____

5. _____

6. _____

7. _____

8. _____

9. _____

10. _____

Look over your goals. Which ones are concrete and specific? Which ones are more vague or hard to define? Consider whether each goal is short-term or longterm. You can put an S next to the short-term ones and an L next to the long-term ones.

Checkpoint

Do you have at least a few short-term and long-term goals?

Yes _____ No _____

If you have only one or two goals, give it some time. Try to think for a few minutes each day about what you want to accomplish in the next few days, weeks, or months. What do you want to accomplish in the next six months or the next year? Having only one or two goals is not a problem if you're clear what they are and you really value them. However, if you have only one or two goals because you're not used to thinking about planning and pursuing goals, it will take a little practice to begin thinking in a goal-oriented way.

Exercise: How to Accomplish Short-Term Goals

Here are six manageable steps to achieving short-term goals:

1. Clearly define the goal.

2. Identify the steps necessary to achieve the goal.

3. Arrange the steps in a logical order.

4. Make a commitment to each step.

5. Take the step, no matter what your mood is like.

6. Pat yourself on the back after each step is completed.

The first thing you need to do is choose one or two short-term goals and define them clearly. Look over your list of goals and choose one short-term goal. Consider it carefully and ask yourself how well the goal is defined. Will you know when you've accomplished it? You may need to rework the goal somewhat to more clearly define it. Once you feel that your goal is clear, write it down in the space below:

Short-term goal number 1 _____

_____

Now you need to consider what steps are necessary to achieve the goal. Don't worry about the order of the steps at this point. Just think of as many steps as you can that need to be completed. Try to avoid combining several different steps into one big step that's difficult to accomplish. Write down the steps you think of in the space below:

_____

_____

_____

_____

_____

_____

Now think about a logical order for the steps. What needs to happen first? Are there some steps that require others to be completed first? If not, try to start with the easiest step, so you can quickly have a sense of progress. Write down an order for the steps below. There's space for eight steps. If you don't need all eight, leave some blank. If you need more, write them on a separate piece of paper.

1. _____

2. _____

3. _____

4. _____

5. _____

6. _____

7. _____

8. _____

Now it's time to make a commitment to step number 1. Commit to a day and time to begin step 1. Then, no matter what your mood is like, begin working on it. If you are unable to finish step 1, make another commitment to continue with it at a specific time in the future. Some people find it helpful to make a multiday or multiweek commitment. For example, if your goal was to spend at least one day of every weekend doing something fun outdoors, the first step might be doing some research to find activities. You might make the commitment to spend one hour between 8:00 and 9:00 P.M. every other night for a week researching and planning activities. Below is a space to write down your initial commitment to take the first step. (Make written commitments for each subsequent step on a separate sheet of paper, but only after you complete the step that precedes it.)

Commitment to step 1: _____

_____

Place a check mark next to each step after completing it. Then, make sure to congratulate yourself and give yourself credit for what you've accomplished, no matter how small. Don't fall into the trap of saying to yourself, "Oh, that was easy. No big deal. I should have been able to do that a long time ago." Remember, you're working on self-activation because you're finding it difficult get back to engagement in your life. That means it's not easy to do these things. It's hard. If you've completed one of the steps toward your goal, it's worth giving yourself some credit.

Below is an example of a short-term goal plan completed by Maggie. Maggie had been depressed for at least six months and spent a great deal of time worrying about getting her house in order. Below is her short-term plan for getting her basement cleaned out. Following her plan, there is a blank goal planning worksheet that you can photocopy and use for other short-term goals you want to achieve.

Maggie's Short-Term Goal Planning Worksheet

1. Short-term goal: *Clean out the basement because it's been bugging me for over a year.*

2. Steps toward the goal: *Wash floor and walls; clean windows; have a garage sale; buy a dehumidifier; open all the boxes, look through everything, sort into piles to throw away, keep, or sell; move piles to one side of basement.*

3. Order of the steps:

    1. *Open all the boxes, look through everything, sort into piles to throw away, keep, or sell.*

    2. *Move piles to one side of basement.*

    3. *Wash floor and walls; clean windows.*

    4. *Have a garage sale.*

    5. *Buy a dehumidifier.*

4. Initial commitment to step 1: *I will spend one hour, from eight to nine, each night for the next three nights, sorting things in the basement into piles.*

Your Short-Term Goal Planning Worksheet

1. Short-term goal: _____

_____

2. Steps toward the goal:

_____

_____

_____

_____

_____

_____

_____

3. Order of the steps:

    1. _____

    2. _____

    3. _____

    4. _____

    5. _____

    6. _____

    7. _____

    8. _____

4. Initial commitment to step 1: _____

_____

_____

Exercise: Achieving Your Goals

Over the next several weeks, put your short-term goal plans into action and see what you can accomplish. As you're making progress, observe your mood, but don't let it control your behavior. Although acting independently of your mood may not be a magic cure for your depression, most people find that as they accomplish what they set out to do, they feel a much greater sense of control over their lives, and their mood improves.

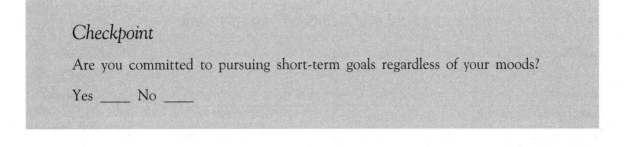

Checkpoint

Are you committed to pursuing short-term goals regardless of your moods?

Yes _____ No _____

What Are Your Long-Term Goals?

If you're like most people, when you were a child, you probably thought about what you wanted to be when you grew up. The first time you thought about this was probably the first time you considered your long-term goals. Long-term goals are those things you would like to have happen in the future and that take more than a few weeks or months to achieve. Below are some examples of long-term goals:

- having a larger group of friends

- being involved in a long-term relationship

- changing jobs or careers

- buying your own home

- becoming less vulnerable to depression in the future

- publishing a book or a screenplay

You can see how long-term goals are related to short-term goals. For example, if you had the long-term goal of buying your own home, some shorter term goals might include exploring different strategies for saving money, gathering information on neighborhoods and prices of homes, checking out loan options, and so forth. Each of these short-term goals would move you closer to the long-term goal. Therefore, achieving long-term goals is really a matter of deciding on the short-term goals necessary to get there, and then committing to each one. But first, you need to have a sense of what your long-term goals are.

Exercise: Looking Ahead

Take some time to think about the next few years in your life. What would you like to be different? What do you want to accomplish? It can be helpful to think of goals in different areas of life, such as family, intimate relationships, work, finances, health, and so on. Some goals will take longer than others to accomplish. For now, think about goals anywhere from the next six months to five years from now. Don't be afraid to set your goals high. The idea is to give yourself the freedom to consider what you value and what you want in your life.

In the space below write down as many long-term goals as you can. For now, leave the columns on the right side (labeled R and D) blank.

Your Long-Term Goals   R   D

1. _____   _____   _____

2. _____   _____   _____

3. _____   _____   _____

4. _____   _____   _____

5. _____   _____   _____

6. _____   _____   _____

7. _____   _____   _____

8. _____   _____   _____

Having Trouble Finding Goals?

You may find it hard to think of long-term goals. If you've been depressed for a long time, you may have forgotten how to think proactively about the future. Instead of thinking, "What do I want and how can I get there?" you may be thinking something like, "I have no hope that things will improve in the future, so why bother?" It may take a bit of practice to come up with long-term goals. Remember not to let your mood control how you behave. Commit to coming up with goals, regardless of how you feel.

Bringing Dreams into the Limits of the Real World

Take a look at your goals. What do you notice? Which goals stand out in either a positive or a negative way? You'll probably see that some goals are more easily achievable than others.

Some may seem way beyond your ability to achieve them, while others may seem much more manageable. Below is an example of some long-term goals that Isaac made for himself.

Isaac's long-term goals	R	D
1. Landscape the entire backyard	3	3
2. Move to the west coast of Ireland	2	5
3. Find a job where I can work outdoors and make a good living	4	4
4. Learn to cook	5	2

Look at the numbers next to each goal under the letters R and D. The letter R stands for "realistic." Isaac asked himself how realistic each goal was and rated it on a scale from 1 (not at all realistic) to 5 (very realistic). Realistic means that the goal is something Isaac could achieve given the reality of his life situation. For example, moving to the west coast of Ireland was not a very realistic goal, since Isaac did not make much money and would have a difficult time finding work as a recent immigrant to another country. Therefore, moving to Ireland got the fairly low score of 2. However, learning to cook received a score of 5 because the goal was well within Isaac's future abilities; all he had to do was take some courses or begin to use cookbooks.

Isaac also considered how desirable each long-term goal was. Under the letter D he rated each goal on a scale of 1 (not at all desirable) to 5 (very desirable). For each goal, the question was, "How much do I want to achieve this goal? How desirable is it to me?" After having rated both how realistic and how desirable each goal was, it was easy for Isaac to see which goals he wanted to pursue. Those that were only somewhat realistic and somewhat desirable, such as landscaping the backyard, were not as important to Isaac as those that were both realistic and desirable (finding a job where he could work outdoors and make a good living).

Exercise: Evaluating Your Goals

Now look again at each of your long-term goals. Ask yourself how realistic and how desirable each goal is. Will you have the resources to achieve particular goals? Are they goals that you will value in your life? Rate each goal on a scale of 1 (not at all) to 5 (very) in terms of how realistic and desirable the goal is. After evaluating each long-term goal, you may want to change some of them. For example, Isaac realized that the goal of "find a job where I can work outdoors" wasn't very realistic because he needed to make a good living. Therefore, he changed to goal to "find a job where I can work outdoors and make a good living." Some of your own goals may need to be scaled back or made larger depending on how realistic or desirable they are. Below is a space for you to write your revised goals if you need to.

Your Revised Long-Term Goals   R   D

1. _____   _____   _____

2. _____   _____   _____

3. _____   _____   _____

4. _____   _____   _____

5. _____   _____   _____

6. _____   _____   _____

7. _____   _____   _____

8. _____   _____   _____

GETTING STARTED AND STAYING MOTIVATED

It may feel strange as you begin to pursue your short- and long-term goals when your mood at any moment may be depressed, and you don't feel like doing anything. You may feel like you're being forced by something outside yourself. After all, isn't it *you* who doesn't feel like exercising today? If you go ahead and do it, who's in charge of your behavior?

You can see the dilemma here. On the one hand, no one is really forcing you to pursue your goals. On the other hand, you may have the sense that there is external pressure to perform, and you may want to resist it by not pursuing your goals. If your goals are ones that you personally value, then it is you who ultimately loses out. When you're feeling resistant, one way out of this dilemma is to remind yourself that *you* are the one who benefits from pursuing your goals. Your goals are yours and no one else's. Even if others will approve of your goals, it is your choice whether or not to pursue them. Try saying to yourself something like, "I can choose to resist working toward this goal, or I can choose to pursue it, but either way it is I who am choosing."

Acting "As If"

Most people assume that their feelings and moods cause their behavior. In fact, there is a large body of psychological research showing that the opposite is often true: the way you act determines how you feel (Laird and Bresler 1992). In one study, people were asked to try to keep a pencil lodged between their upper lips and their noses. If you try this, you will see that the only way to do it is to force the lower part of your face into a smile. The people who performed this behavior reported feeling in a better mood following the experiment than people led to frown without being aware of it. The second group reported more feelings of anger (Laird 1974). Neither group knew the purpose of the experiment.

How does this apply to pursuing your short- and long-term goals when you're struggling with depression? The short answer is that acting as if you had the motivation to pursue a particular goal (when your mood tells you otherwise) can actually help generate motivation and help you progress toward a goal. Anna's story illustrates this process.

Becoming involved in a committed relationship with a man was at the top of Anna's long-term goal list. Anna recognized that several short-term goals were necessary first steps. These included such things as socializing more with friends, letting people know that she was single, and possibly initiating get-togethers with men she found interesting. Anna felt stuck because she had no motivation to pursue any of these short-term goals. Every time she thought about asking a coworker out to lunch, for example, she felt hopeless and depressed.

As Anna told a therapist about her situation, the therapist noticed that she behaved a particular way when telling the story. For example, she spoke slowly, in a monotone, and avoided eye contact. The therapist asked Anna, "If you felt confident that you could begin to date and were feeling less depressed, how would you be telling me about this? Tell me about what it will take to begin working on finding a relationship, but show me a confident and less depressed Anna. Don't worry about whether it feels like acting. The whole point is to act differently."

Anna began to make more eye contact with the therapist. She also smiled more as she spoke and sat up straight in her chair. At one point, the therapist stopped her and asked Anna how her mood was right in that moment. To her surprise, Anna noticed that her mood was considerably better than it had been a few minutes ago. It wasn't as if her depression were completely gone, but she certainly felt that she had more motivation and confidence. Soon after her therapy session, Anna began to try acting as if she felt differently whenever she felt stuck in pursuing her goals because of her mood.

Anna even went so far as to attend a party that she dreaded and to act as if she were comfortable and having a good time. She ignored her jittery stomach and fearful thoughts and walked right up to an attractive man to introduce herself. She spent nearly thirty minutes in conversation with this man. He invited her to coffee a few days later and, although they did not become romantically involved, the two established a friendship. Over time she felt less and less depressed and was actively pursuing several goals that she had previously avoided.

If the idea of acting makes you uncomfortable, remember, the goal here is to help yourself gain control over your life and be less dependent on your mood when you're depressed. If acting like you feel differently actually helps you to feel differently and to pursue your own goals, why not do it?

CHAPTER SUMMARY

Moods influence behavior, but they do not cause behavior. You are not doomed to live life simply reacting to every change of mood that you have. Acting according to goals rather than according to a feeling or mood can make you proactive rather than reactive. This chapter, like chapter 6, provided you with ways to break down tasks and goals into manageable parts. Making and pursuing goals, rather than allowing your moods to determine your behavior, is one of the effective ways to end your depression. You have now learned a number of ways to act from the outside in and, as you continue to practice these procedures, should be well on your way to overcoming your depression.

Chapter 8

Build the Life You Want

Recovering from depression is clearly the first step in building a better life. But there is more to life than not feeling depressed. Life involves, among other things, accomplishing the things you wish to accomplish, interacting with the people you love, and living according to your values and beliefs. Although recovering from an episode of depression is a great relief and a significant accomplishment, your ultimate goal probably is to build a life you want to live. Certainly there will always be times in life when you feel down or may even begin to feel depressed. This chapter will focus on building a life that allows you to cope with the down times and to prevent relapse into a full recurrence of depression.

LIFE AFTER DEPRESSION

The chances of being depressed increase with each episode of a major depressive disorder. It is not clear why this is the case, but it may well be that patterns developed during a period of depression become easier to return to when life events make you feel down.

Fighting the Odds Favoring Relapse

You don't need to fear recurrence of depression. It is not a thing that comes upon you in the dark or completely out of the blue, although it certainly can feel that way at times. You may have suffered repeated periods of depression or feel as though you have been depressed your whole life. Using the methods presented in this workbook can help you to avoid relapsing into a full-blown major depressive episode that saps your energy and steals more of your life.

The main point of this book has been to activate you rather than have you succumb to the lethargy that is often a symptom of depression. We've also discussed fighting avoidance, dealing with ruminative thinking, acting "as if," and breaking tasks down into small steps. What this boils down to is that you should develop the habit of being proactive rather than reactive. If you are feeling blue and stay in bed for two-thirds of the day, you are being reactive to a mood. On the other hand, you are being proactive if you are feeling blue, yet you nevertheless approach a few small steps of a planned task. You are also being proactive if you act as though you aren't feeling blue, even if it's just for a short period of the day.

Checkpoint

Do you tend to react to situations that are highly emotionally charged rather than follow through on previous intentions?

Yes _____   No _____

In this chapter you will learn about preventing relapse. You will also learn about applying the principles of self-activation to other issues in your life.

Are You Doomed to Repeat the Past?

One idea that worries so many people who have experienced depression is that they are predisposed to feeling depressed. Family histories of depression can make you fear that you may have a genetic flaw. A life history of loss and abuse can make you think that this may be your lot in life. It can feel like you've always been depressed and that somehow you are simply doomed to remain that way.

History Makes Us Who We Are, But Not Necessarily Who We Will Become

We carry our histories with us wherever we go. You are who you are because of the many experiences of your life, and yet you are much more than that. Once you know that something in your history predisposes you to certain behaviors, you can decide to change those behaviors. Each change you make creates a new history for the future. At each point in your life you are, to some degree, constrained by your past and free to shape your future.

Elizabeth was the second child in a family of three children. Her parents divorced when she was six, leaving her mother with Elizabeth and her two brothers. At the age of nineteen, Elizabeth's older brother, three years older than she, was diagnosed with paranoid schizophrenia. He had always been difficult. He used to lock Elizabeth and the younger brother in the closet to "keep them away from his stuff" or slap Elizabeth in the face for no apparent reason and scream "shut up!" Elizabeth's mother worked long hours and when she was at home tried her best to care for the children. Elizabeth complained about her older brother, but her mother told her that she was certain he was just kidding around and to pay him no attention. Elizabeth's father had little to do with the family. After the divorce, he had moved to a rural town in the northwestern United States. When Elizabeth was sixteen, word came that her father had committed suicide by hanging himself in an abandoned barn.

The erratic behavior of Elizabeth's older brother improved with medication, but he remained at home with her mother and younger brother. As soon as she turned eighteen, Elizabeth moved out of the house and rented a studio apartment while attending community college and working part-time at a clothing store. She completed her associate of arts degree in three years and transferred into a local university. At the university she struggled with the class schedule, and the classes were more difficult than those at the community college she had attended. Although Elizabeth was smart, she was not prepared for the level of work expected of her. She cut her hours at work in half and took out student loans so that she could attend school full-time. She was majoring in biology with the goal of going to medical school. When she received a C average her first quarter, she became discouraged and stopped thinking about medical school.

During the second quarter, Elizabeth began sleeping in and missing her early morning classes. She felt too sad about her poor grades to bother to attend classes. The university was quite large, and nobody seemed to notice that she was missing. She soon stopped attending classes altogether. She also missed enough work to warrant a written warning. The only thing keeping her motivated to go to work was the fear of losing her apartment and having to move back in with her mother and brothers. She began to accept that her time had come to face the "family legacy." Lying in bed at night, she thought about the day when she, too, would commit suicide like her father. She thought she would do it in a more civilized manner than he did. "I may be depressed, but I don't want to die in an old barn," she thought. A friend recommended that she begin therapy, but Elizabeth was reluctant. "Why should I pay money for that? I should have known that I'd get depressed. Look at everyone in my family." After being repeatedly coaxed, however, she called a therapist.

Understandably, Elizabeth made a connection between her past and her current depression. Psychologists would say that they were very likely correlated in some way; in other words, someone with a different history might have reacted differently to the difficulties Elizabeth was experiencing. However, the fact that Elizabeth's past informed her present did not mean that Elizabeth's family biology or her history caused her depression. A combination of life forces was at work. Once she entered therapy and began to discuss her sadness about losing her dream of medical school, Elizabeth began to face her current crisis. Her therapist helped her to get engaged in school again, and Elizabeth managed to keep a C average. In her third quarter, she started taking sociology classes and focusing on the social sciences instead of premed classes. She loved her classes and started getting As for the first time at the university. Eventually Elizabeth recovered her grade point average, took the Graduate Record Examination, and entered a Ph.D. program in sociology. After graduate school, she got a teaching position at a small liberal arts college several states away from her home state. Although she continued to feel down at times, when work was difficult or a relationship did not work out, she remained depression free.

Reopening Old Wounds through the Power of Words

One of the reasons that people believe that negative experiences in the past will continue to haunt them is that reminders of past events are often associated with feelings nearly as strong as the original experience. People make associations. All five senses can function to bring up certain emotions. The smell of a baking pie may remind you of comfort, the sound of a distant train may make you feel lonely.

You know that there are many triggers for depression and triggers for avoidance patterns. Did you know that the words you use might serve as a trigger? Think of the words "dead dog." If you have ever had a dog that died, you may feel a twinge when you read those words. Or you may be reminded of your best friend's last few days. Words are evocative, and your personal history gives certain words greater power. This doesn't mean that you should be leery of using certain words. It is simply a reminder that the things you say evoke memories, images, and feelings, even when they are not directly related to a past event.

How to Think about the Role of Your Parents

Every time Carmella's mother grounded her for not being home within five minutes of her curfew, Carmella thought, "When I have kids, I'll never treat them like this." Kenny, who never wanted kids, made a vow to himself never to sip away at a couple of martinis every evening after work this way his dad did. These people wanted to refrain from making mistakes similar to those of their parents. Parents can also be positive role models, and you may want to follow in their footsteps. Whether you had wonderful parents or miserable parents or parents who were somewhere in between, you will have your own challenges to face that differ from theirs.

Make Your Life about What You Value

Genetics may play a great role in determining the color of your hair and eyes, or certain aspects of your temperament, but it cannot predict precisely how you will act in most situations. Your family genetic history may make you an unlikely candidate for winning a Nobel Prize, but hard work, determination, and having a particular combination of DNA that makes you distinct from the rest of your family can all work in your favor. In short, nothing about where you come from can make it certain that you will think, feel, or behave in particular ways. Uncertainty is built into the system of life. And it's important to remember that you have choices.

Your biological predispositions and your history with people, words, and ideas inform those choices. Consider behaviors that you observed in your parents or loved ones when you were growing up. Many behaviors may have irritated you and you now want to refrain from copying them. Other behaviors you may have admired and wanted to imitate. Recognizing how others once acted when you see it in your own behavior can be a great cue for making a change rather than for feeling that you have to accept a certain fate. If you believe your behavior resembles authority figures you would rather not emulate, try to aspire to either act in accord with their good qualities rather than their bad, or act like someone else altogether, someone whom you admired.

Exercise: The Power of Words

Take a moment and read each word on the list below. Don't read the list too quickly. The words have been picked at random. Pay attention to each word and to the images, memories, or feelings evoked by it. Notice how there is a feeling tone to the word. What images, associations, or feelings does it bring up for you?

farm	ugly	mistake	flowers
mother	simple	daddy	anger
paintbrush	sunshine	brilliant	grandma
death	stupid	energy	uncle
chocolate	lazy	absent	vomit
brat	grease	liberate	odor
ecstasy	glue	fluffy	fat
teacher	Christmas	beach	beauty
knife	wind	Hanukkah	blood

What does this tell you about the power of words to create and maintain moods?

_____

_____

_____

_____

_____

_____

_____

Words and images can be evocative. Often, this is an explanation for why certain feelings seem to come over you suddenly. You may not recognize the connection between hearing a song or a story on the radio and feeling blue, but sad feelings can be triggered by something occurring without your noticing what it is. As a result, you might be convinced that there is something wrong with you. In fact, you are feeling something that was actually elicited by your environment, whether or not you can put your finger on the words, stories, or ideas that elicited the feeling. Be aware of this when you suddenly feel a change in your mood for better or worse, and don't think that you are inherently doomed to feel depressed at random.

Exercise: What Behaviors Do
You Wish Not to Imitate?

List below several behaviors you observed in others as you grew up that you have told yourself you will never do.

_____

_____

_____

_____

_____

_____

_____

Now that you have listed some behaviors you want to avoid, the trick is not to avoid them but to actively do the opposite. Rather than spending a lot of energy trying not to do something, it's more effective to strive for something positive.

Say an authority figure from your youth had a bad temper and often harassed you with such statements as, "Quit that crying or I'll give you something to cry about!" You might wish not to repeat behavior of this sort.

You can certainly choose to avoid such phrases. But what happens if a child, a friend, or a coworker makes you angry? Biting your tongue will probably be ineffective in the long run if the situation continues, yet you may be afraid of losing your cool.

The opposite of losing your cool is to take reasoned action. With a child, for example, you might try calmly stating your feelings by saying, "When you misbehave like that, it makes me very angry." You might also try portioning out discipline according to how serious the misbehavior is rather than according to how mad your child's behavior made you. You can see from this example that proactively engaging in an opposite action can be much more effective than thinking only about avoiding behaviors you don't want to engage in.

On the other hand, you may wish to act similarly to your parents or other authority figures in your life, yet, as in Lilly's case, the circumstances of your life may be quite different. Let's say you would like to emulate the behavior of a previous schoolteacher who was kind to students and skilled at teaching, but you do not teach for a living. You would need to determine more specifically what it was about the teacher that so impressed you and then figure out how act similarly.

Exercise: What Behaviors Do You Respect?

Below, list several behaviors that you respect in others and would like to engage in yourself:

_____

_____

_____

_____

_____

_____

The trick now is to find ways to apply behaviors that you observed in circumstances different from your own situation. Take the example of the schoolteacher. She or he may have been soft-spoken yet firm, always willing to assist others, a good listener, and entertaining; these are all behaviors that you can exhibit in a variety of work, family, and social situations. Even if you never have the opportunity to teach formally, you can keep an open-door policy, be available to listen to coworkers, friends, or family, and offer advice as needed.

Whether you are acting in ways opposite to those you observed or are imitating a good example, you are acting according to something that you value. We all have opportunities to model our lives after certain people, real or fictional. You may even wish to follow a particular ideal or value that has always been important to you. For example, it may be important to you to be a generous person. Being a generous person doesn't mean that you would give away all your goods and constantly be doling out money and gifts to others. It does mean, however, that you would value offering your time, your money, or other gifts as much as possible in appropriate situations. This would be an ideal that you value, or a behavior that you model.

It Is Easier to Do Something Than to Avoid Doing Something Else

Procrastinating is an extremely common behavior that many people spend a great deal of time trying to talk themselves out of. If you tell yourself "don't procrastinate," what does that leave for you to do? Having read this book, you know that telling yourself to "do something" is too vague. However, telling yourself to "walk around the block," "wash the glasses and silverware," "type one paragraph on the page," and so on are all steps away from procrastination. They are positive steps.

This is also true with larger life issues. Make a plan for how you want to be. Take that plan and break it down into components that you can do in a step-by-step fashion. Now try to do the behaviors that you have chosen. Before you know it, you'll be living a life that you desire and, at the same time, will not be repeating patterns from the past or re-creating the bad habits that your family, teachers, neighbors, or others had.

PROBLEM-SOLVING

In chapter 5 we discussed the power of rumination in keeping you depressed. As a reminder, researchers have found that people who think and worry about their problems without actively working toward solutions tend to be more severely depressed and tend to stay depressed longer than those who are actively solving problems (Lyubomirsky and Nolen-Hoeksema 1995). Learning to take an active problem-solving approach to life issues is another way to beat depression and to combat relapse.

Name It, Know It, and Solve It

When you feel physically ill, it helps to have a doctor define what is wrong with you so that you can find relief or even a cure. When all you know is that you have an aching stomach, there isn't much you can do but eat bland food and wait it out. If the doctor tells you that an ulcer is the cause of your aching stomach, you have several options for dealing with it. You would want to educate yourself about ulcers and choose the best solution for you. This is the case with other problems in life. If you can name them and understand them better, you are more likely to be able to solve them.

Earlier in this chapter we talked about the myth of history as an explanatory cause. You don't necessarily need to know why something is a problem, but you should understand what the problem is. "What" questions are always more helpful than "why" questions. Asking why dogs walk on four legs rather than two is less helpful than understanding that your dog is going to teeter over and fall if you hold his front paws in the air and make him stand on his back legs only. Thus, to work out solutions to your problems, you need to define the problems carefully and clearly, understand the context in which you must work out your solutions, and develop strategies for solving the problems or coping with them.

Exercise: Making a Vague Problem More Concrete

Look at the problem below. Imagine that this is something that you experience. Try to write a definition in concrete, behavioral terms.

Problem: "I feel blah all the time and don't enjoy anything."

Write your concrete, behavioral definition here: _____

_____

_____

_____

_____

_____

Here's one way that a person might concretely define feeling blah all the time and not enjoying anything: "I spend too much time in bed, and avoid calling my friends. I don't engage in activities that I used to enjoy because I don't take pleasure in them. I feel sad and think sad thoughts most of the day."

Vagueness is your enemy, especially when you are depressed. If you went to work for an employer who told you on your first day, "Sit in this room and do some work," you'd be rather concerned about what you were being asked to do. You might even feel a little anxious. The lack of direction could be overwhelming. On a new job, you expect a boss to show you what he or she expects of you and to explain your job in direct terms. It helps to describe problems in behavioral terms. If you know specifically what the problem is, you can more easily develop the steps toward a solution.

Exercise: Defining a Problem You Would Like to Solve

Take this time to write a definition for a problem you may still be experiencing. Remember to write concretely.

_____

_____

_____

_____

_____

_____

Brainstorming Solutions

Brainstorming is a method of generating as many solutions to a problem as possible without stopping to evaluate whether each solution is likely to be helpful. This is an important first step that you may skip when trying to solve a problem. Instead, you may generate one idea at a time and get stuck evaluating an idea before all the possible solutions are on the table. As a result, you may conclude prematurely that a problem can't be solved. It's much better to generate as many ideas as possible, and then go back and consider the pros and cons of each solution.

As an example, say that the man who occupies the cubicle next to you at work talks very loudly on the telephone, and it disturbs your own conversations and makes it difficult for you to concentrate. When you brainstorm solutions, you come up with the following:

- Move your cubicle.

- Tear out his telephone.

- Start talking really loud yourself, so he'll notice.

- Speak to him about the problem.

- Speak with your supervisor about the problem.

- Quit your job.

When you review your list, you quickly notice that the first two solutions have more cons than pros. You cannot move your cubicle without permission from your supervisor, and it is a drastic measure that doesn't guarantee that your next neighbor will be any better. The second solution obviously would work against you; you might be reprimanded or fired for tearing out a phone. It also would serve as a rage response, reducing your frustration for a moment but causing more problems in the long run. In other words, the first two solutions are simply avoidance maneuvers. The third solution is very indirect and relies too heavily on your coworker's ability to notice your behavior and understand what it is intended to communicate.

The third and fourth solutions have more advantages. In fact, you can combine them to make a good solution to the problem. First, speak to your coworker directly. If he is not responsive, discuss the situation with your supervisor. Finally, the last solution, to quit your job, has obvious disadvantages; you would be hurting yourself in an attempt to make life better.

Try not to make the mistake of rejecting ideas before you have thought about them. In the coworker example, it may have been fun and given you a bit of a chuckle to include "take a soft rubber mallet to work and bonk him on the head every time he answers the phone." This is obviously a ridiculous solution, but it contains the grain of truth that finding a way to alert your coworker when he is loud might be useful. If you immediately rejected the idea from your brainstorming, this bit of information would be lost.

Carrying Out the Solution

Of course, developing an idea for a solution to a problem does no good unless you act on it. Since you will need to carry out the solutions you plan, make sure that they are realistic and are either within your comfort zone or are only far enough from your comfort zone to be a reasonable challenge. Solutions to life problems that involve changing the world or moving mountains are not reasonable solutions.

When you work on solving problems, there is no need to keep trying the same solution over and over again if it is not working. Set a time when you will evaluate the results. In the example above, if you chose to talk with your coworker, you could set a date for doing so, talk to him, and then allow two weeks to see if his behavior changes. If he was receptive but still speaks loudly, you might give him a gentle reminder. So during the two-week trial period, you'd remind him once, and then evaluate your solution.

Testing Outcomes

When you are depressed, you may find yourself giving up and losing heart very easily. Therefore, it is essential that you consider problem solving to be a hypothesis-testing process. This means that you define the problem, brainstorm solutions, decide on a particular solution, carry it out, and test the results to see if it worked to resolve the problem at hand. Using the example of the loud coworker again, does he actually begin to talk more quietly on the telephone? Does he show you consideration? If yes, you have solved the problem. If not, then you need to try another solution from the brainstorming list or completely rethink the solution.

Rethinking the Solution

If you have exhausted the solutions on your brainstorming list, you may need to brainstorm some more. Testing solutions and not succeeding may also give you ideas for how to redefine the problem. You can simply go back to the beginning and try again. Most scientific experiments fail initially, which is why scientists will often conduct pilot studies before engaging in costly experiments. Pilot studies allow investigators to see flaws or difficulties in conducting experiments. If necessary, they will return to their original research question and rethink ways to answer it. Finding solutions to the problems in life is not that much different. Successful people usually have a history of trying things, succeeding at some, failing at others, but always moving forward by attempting to solve problems.

WHAT ABOUT PROBLEMS THAT HAVE NO OBVIOUS SOLUTION?

Not all problems in life have solutions. You may have to live with some things that you can't change. Activation therapy is also about making your life better even if there are things that you don't feel good about.

Accepting the Things You Cannot Change

Although you certainly have control over how you react to situations, or how you respond to your reactions, you may not have control over the situations themselves. Part of recovering from depression and building a better life is recognizing that striving to fix everything in your life can, at times, make things worse. In academic settings, where behavior therapy continues to develop and change, acceptance has become an integral part of treatment (Hayes, Strosahl, and Wilson 1999). Life comes with suffering as well as with joy and happiness. Accepting only those things that make you feel good is simply not accepting life.

It is also important to recognize that acceptance is not the same as resignation. Acceptance is not furrowing your brow and saying to yourself, "Fine, if that's the way it has to be, then that's the way it has to be." Approaching problems this way creates a sort of pseudo-acceptance in which you are still emotionally attached to a problem and trying to control it by not controlling it. True acceptance is more of a genuine willingness to give up the struggle to control things that you can't control. It is a skill that takes quite a bit of practice.

Relying on the Kindness of Others

It is easier to accept the adversities of life when you have a strong support network. If you find yourself withdrawing from friends, it is time to get reconnected and break the pattern. You may think, "But my friends are tired of hearing how miserable I am." There may be some truth in this, if all you tell your friends is that you feel hopeless and that you are miserable. However, when you are struggling with things in your life, and you turn to your friends for solace and advice, they will typically support you. It is important to stay connected to others, not only when you are depressed but also when you are working on building a rewarding life and preventing a relapse of depression. Unfortunately, when you are depressed, you most likely underestimate yourself, and you probably underestimate the concern available from your friends and loved ones.

Self-Soothing in the Absence of Companionship

Of course, it is not always possible to be in the presence of others. Sometimes it's even difficult to stay connected over the phone, through e-mail, or by writing letters. If you are elderly and have outlived most of your family or friends, or if you are living far away from friends and family, or if you are socially anxious and have difficulty connecting with people, you may find it difficult to establish a support network. You will need to soothe yourself through rough times when you face problems that are not easily solved or are perhaps unsolvable.

Self-soothing is different from self-anesthesia, and the methods you use to soothe should not be avoidance maneuvers. An example of an avoidance strategy masquerading as self-soothing is drinking alcohol or abusing other substances. After a rough day, having several alcoholic drinks to calm down is basically avoidance, because it is a way to numb yourself. Self-soothing means remaining engaged in your life and treating yourself well.

There are many ways to soothe yourself. You might simply settle into a comfortable chair, have a cup of tea, and reminisce about happier times. Or you might take a walk by a river, go fishing, or work in the garden. Everyone is different, and you can be creative with strategies for soothing yourself. The word "soothe" can have many different meanings as well. It can mean to calm, to heal, to please, to comfort, or even to enjoy. You can use the exercise below to help you develop a menu of ways to soothe yourself.

Exercise: Self-Soothing through Your Senses

In times of distress, your five senses can come to your aid. In this exercise make a list of things that could give you pleasure or have a calming effect.

Sight: List things that you enjoy seeing. Try to gather as great a variety of visual images as possible that you can use when feeling blue. Consider nature, art, and architecture. List things that you can look at on a walk, in the comfort of your home, and so on.

_____

_____

_____

_____

_____

Sound: You may enjoy listening to music. What other sounds please you? List a variety of sounds that can help you engage in life and feel enjoyment or solace. You can list sounds that are created electronically or sounds that exist in nature. Think of everyday sounds that may be comforting for you.

_____

_____

_____

_____

_____

Touch: The sense of touch can be very powerful. For example, the feel of warm water on your body in the form of a bath or shower can be a pleasant sensation. What are the things you can touch and feel that can turn a lonely moment into an opportunity to experience something pleasurable?

_____

_____

_____

_____

_____

Smell: There are many scents in the world that you may respond to positively. Think of the aroma of the air after a cool rain. You don't need to spend money to activate your sense of smell. List some things below that you enjoy smelling and find soothing.

_____

_____

_____

_____

_____

Taste: Depending on your weight and general health, eating rich, fatty foods may not be a good choice for self-soothing. However, there are many tastes in the world that you can enjoy without risk to your health or self-esteem. Occasional indulgence may also help you feel special. List some things you enjoy eating or tasting and that you find soothing.

_____

_____

_____

_____

_____

Now that you have a menu of things to see, hear, touch, smell and taste, choose some of the things from the menu and experiment. You may find that you can indulge several senses at once. Take in the entire experience.

COPING WITH DIFFICULT FEELINGS

Keeping yourself free of mood-dependent behavior can keep you advancing toward larger goals in your life. Here are some suggestions for how to cope with some common distressing emotions.

Feeling	How to Cope
Overwhelmed	Break a task down into smaller components.
Fearful	Do the least frightening steps first and move up a hierarchy to the scarier steps.
Bored	Make the situation more interesting externally (play music you like, etc.)
Tired	Reward yourself frequently during a boring or tiring task. Take breaks.
Angry	Relax and concentrate on something that you're not as frustrated with.
Sad	Allow yourself to feel the sadness for a while. There is no reason to stifle it, especially if you are grieving over a loss. When you feel sad all of the time, however, try to let it go. Crying can be a good release, so listen to a favorite song or watch a sad movie. Once you've cried it out, try to do something constructive. Talk to someone else, and focus the conversation on something other than your sadness.

CHAPTER SUMMARY

Self-activation can help you get closer to having the life you want. Be sure to set reasonable goals, understand your limitations, and move forward gradually. You may need to self-activate while feeling hurt or disappointed over the past. You may need to spend some time defining problems, brainstorming solutions, and testing them out. You may also need to soothe and comfort yourself along the way. The ultimate goal is to remain engaged with your life so that you will not miss opportunities that come your way.

Chapter 9

Tying It All Together

Now that you're nearing the end of this workbook, this chapter begins with a series of exercises that will help you get a sense of the bigger picture. What have you learned about yourself? In general, how is your mood now compared to when you started this workbook? Are you considering additional treatment options at this point? People often wonder about the effectiveness of combining different treatments for depression. In fact, combined treatments are not uncommon. The rest of the chapter considers other approaches to working with depression and how you might integrate them into a self-activation approach.

WHERE HAVE YOU BEEN AND WHERE ARE YOU NOW?

Take some time to think about where you were in your life when you began working on self-activation. How was your mood on average? What sorts of things were happening in your life that either brought you pleasure or caused you stress? How were you spending most of your days and evenings?

Think about where you are in your life now. How is your mood on average? What sorts of things are happening in your life that bring you pleasure or cause you stress? How are you spending most of your days and evenings? This is the sort of perspective that will help give you a sense of where you're at in your work on ending depression. Below are some exercises that will help you clarify the picture.

Exercise: How's Your Depression Now?

Use a scale of 1 to 10 to rate on average how bad your depression has been over the last month, over the last week, and over the last couple of days. A score of 1 indicates that you have had no feelings of depression. A score of 10 indicates that the depression you've been experiencing is the worst you've ever experienced. A score of 5 indicates that you have been moderately depressed. Fill in the blanks.

 ◆ "Over the last month, my depression has been at a level of ___ ."

 ◆ "Over the last week, my depression has been at a level of ___ ."

 ◆ "Over the last couple of days, my depression has been at a level of ___ ."

What do you notice? If the numbers you entered seem to be going down from the last month to the last couple of days, then it probably means that your mood is improving. If the numbers stayed roughly the same, it could mean that your depression has not changed and continues to be a problem. Or, if they've stayed the same but remained low it may mean that you've been feeling steadily better over the last month.

Exercise: What's Happening in Your Life Now?

In the space below, write down the things happening in your life now that either bring you pleasure or cause you stress. Place a plus sign next to those things that bring you pleasure and a minus sign next to those that cause you stress. For example, after eight weeks of working on self-activation, Jason wrote down the following:

 1. *Started dating a woman I really like* (+)

 2. *Getting more accomplished at work* (+)

 3. *Still dealing with the aftermath of the divorce* (-)

What's happening in your life?

1. _____

2. _____

3. _____

4. _____

5. _____

6. _____

Exercise: How Helpful Has Behavioral Activation Been for You?

On the scale below, rate how helpful engaging in behavioral activation has been for you. Consider how much your mood has changed, what's happening in your life right now, how hopeful you feel about the future now compared to when you started working on activation, and any other changes that are important to you.

Self-activation has been (circle one):

1	2	3	4
Not at all helpful	A little helpful	Helpful	Extremely helpful

Now, look at your score and consider why you rated the helpfulness of activation the way that you did. In the space below, write down the reasons that behavioral activation was helpful or not helpful. For example, if you thought activation was a little helpful, you could write down *how* it was a little helpful, and also why it wasn't more helpful or extremely helpful. Below is an example from Christina who found self-activation to be helpful.

Reasons why Christina rated activation as helpful:

1. *It gave me something to do other than sit and think about all my problems.*

2. *I was able to get back in touch with friends, which has really improved my mood.*

3. *I'm exercising now, which makes me feel better about myself.*

4. *I wouldn't consider it extremely helpful because I still get depressed once in a while. However, the periods don't last nearly as long as they did, and I have a good idea of how to deal with them when they happen.*

Reasons why you rated activation as you did:

1. _____

2. _____

3. _____

4. _____

5. _____

Exercise: What Have You Learned about Yourself?

It's often useful to consider what you've learned about yourself after you've spent some time making changes in your life. This can help you remember the sorts of changes that have a positive effect on your mood, so if you ever become depressed again you'll have a good idea where to begin and how to start working on it.

Since starting self-activation, perhaps you've learned which activities or interactions with others are particularly enjoyable for you. Maybe you've learned something about the most common ways you tend to respond when you feel sad or depressed. Perhaps you've noticed particular areas in your life, such as intimate relationships, friendships, family, or leisure time, that need more attention. These are just a handful of possibilities. In the space below, write down some things you have learned about yourself through working on self-activation:

1. _____

2. _____

3. _____

4. _____

5. _____

Exercise: Which Changes in Your Behavior Have Had the Most Positive Effect on Your Mood?

Now think about what changes in your behavior have had a positive effect on your mood. Can you list the changes that have had the greatest effect? What are they?

_____

_____

_____

_____

_____

_____

WHERE ARE YOU HEADED FROM HERE?

Now that you have taken a step back and looked at where you've been, it's time to consider where you're going from here. Do you still need to work on ending depression? Do you feel like you're back to your normal self? Are you considering seeking some professional help? Are there other issues in your life that you need to deal with?

Hopefully, you've found that self-activation is a simple, yet powerful tool. You can continue to use the exercises in this workbook daily, weekly, or once every few months as a means of tuning up your skills. Self-activation can be used alone or in combination with other tools that you can either learn on your own or with professional help. The rest of this chapter addresses how you can use behavioral activation strategies in combination with other approaches to overcoming depression.

Many people find it useful to work on making changes in their lives with the help of a professional therapist. If you are currently in therapy and have been finding this workbook helpful, consider discussing it with your therapist if you haven't done so already. If you would like to find a therapist to work with you on behavioral activation, you may want to search for someone who describes their orientation as behavioral or cognitive behavioral. You can also look for referrals on the Web site of the Association for the Advancement of Behavior Therapy (AABT), an international organization of researchers and clinicians specializing in behavior therapy. Membership in organizations such as AABT suggest that a therapist is interested in and has some skill in behavior therapy or cognitive behavioral therapy. There are also certifying bodies that examine the competence of therapists in these specialties. For psychologists, the American Board of Behavioral Psychology serves as the primary certifying body. The Academy of Cognitive Therapy also certifies practitioners from a variety of fields in cognitive therapy.

SELF-ACTIVATION AND OTHER TREATMENT OPTIONS

People often wonder whether self-activation approaches can be used along with other common treatments for depression. The answer is yes. As we discussed at the beginning of the workbook, there are a number of other approaches to working on depression that have been studied and found to be effective. Some of these approaches actually use a number of behavioral activation techniques.

One word of caution: With the exception of cognitive therapy, behavioral activation in combination with other treatment approaches has not been fully studied. While we have little reason to think that a combined approach could be harmful, we do agree with many other clinical psychologists and researchers that the best approach is to first try recognized treatments that have solid scientific support. On the other hand, you may have tried one or more of these scientific treatments with limited positive results and are interested in combining them with behavioral activation to see if you can get better results. With this in mind, below you will find information about other treatments for depression and how they might be combined with a self-activation approach.

Cognitive Therapy

Cognitive therapy (Beck et al. 1979) is probably the most well-studied psychotherapy for depression. Research has shown that the treatment is effective compared to no treatment at all, and there is some evidence that it is more effective than antidepressant medication (Gloaguen et al. 1998). Two studies have directly compared behavioral activation to cognitive therapy. The first (Jacobson et al. 1996) found no differences in effectiveness between the treatments. The second study (Dimidjian et al. 2003) included comparisons to antidepressant medication and a pill placebo. After sixteen weeks of treatment, the results showed that for moderately to severely depressed patients, behavioral activation was more effective than cognitive therapy or medication. At a two-year, posttreatment follow-up, no differences in effectiveness were found with the three treatments. In other words, behavioral activation, cognitive therapy, and medication all prevented relapse at about the same rate.

Cognitive therapy proceeds from the assumption that the way people think about events in their lives affects their mood. When people are depressed, they are more likely to interpret events negatively and to see events as reflections of personal weaknesses or flaws (Beck et al. 1979). Thus, much of cognitive therapy is spent teaching people to increase their awareness of their own negative thinking. Once a person is aware of what they are thinking and how it affects their mood, the therapy introduces strategies for learning to think in more neutral terms. For example, if a woman held the belief, "I must be perfect to be loved by others," she might interpret a critical comment from a friend or loved one as reflecting poorly on her own self-worth. Cognitive therapy would help her to look at the situation differently; perhaps she would ask herself, "What else could the comment mean? Why else might the person have said it? What evidence is there that I need to be perfect?"

As it turns out, cognitive therapy uses quite a bit of behavioral activation but in a somewhat different way. During the early stages of therapy, people are encouraged to schedule and structure activities into their lives that bring them a sense of pleasure or mastery (Beck et al. 1979). These activation techniques generally are used in the early stages of treatment to help people challenge negative thoughts. For example, if you thought, "I'm incapable of getting anything done," you might schedule some simple chores to do on a particular day. If you completed the chores, this would be seen as evidence that the thought "I'm incapable of getting anything done" is not entirely accurate.

Interestingly, research has shown that most of the change in depression that people experience during cognitive therapy tends to occur during the first few sessions, in which activation techniques play more of a role (Jacobson et al. 1996). These findings were part of the reason researchers began to develop behavioral activation as a treatment on its own.

Can Cognitive Therapy Be Combined with Behavioral Activation?

It is possible to combine cognitive therapy and behavioral activation. You might simply use techniques from both treatments without worrying about which treatment is "right," what causes depression, or the best way to end depression. For example, you might find that identifying TRAPs is particularly helpful for you and also that challenging your negative thinking helps you to approach rather than avoid difficult situations. Or, if it's important to you to stick to one way of understanding depression, you might include techniques from cognitive therapy into behavioral activation.

You should be careful about a couple of things when you combine techniques from different treatment approaches. First, you don't want to overcomplicate things by trying several different techniques at once. If you do this, you may find it difficult to use any of the techniques to their full potential. Second, as discussed above, you don't want to get stuck trying to figure out which approach is the correct approach. For example, if you've found behavioral activation to be helpful, and you now find cognitive techniques also to be helpful, both can be helpful to you. There's no reason to choose just one approach.

Some people find it useful to use cognitive techniques within a self-activation framework. For example, imagine that you are in the middle of completing a particular task that you scheduled for yourself. As you're working on the task, you become gradually more depressed as you slip into ruminating about a particular problem in your life. Once you recognize the ruminating, you have several options. You could attend to your experience, or you could continue to follow through with the task regardless of what you're feeling at the time, or you could try identifying errors in your thinking that are worsening your mood (cognitive therapy). One approach might work well for you in one situation while another approach may be more helpful in a different situation.

Insight-Oriented Therapies

Insight-oriented therapies emphasize the importance of understanding how unconscious feelings, wishes, fears, and beliefs cause you to feel depressed. People will often also explore how difficult or painful childhood experiences have contributed to the problems they are experiencing. Although there are a wide variety of insight-oriented or psychodynamic approaches, they all proceed roughly from the same set of assumptions. The first is that all people experience unconscious conflicts that are often rooted in childhood. These conflicts may have to do with such things as relationships and intimacy, anger or fear, sexual issues, or a range of other issues.

The second assumption is that many mental-health problems are the result of ongoing attempts by people to prevent unconscious conflicts from surfacing. For example, you might be experiencing a great deal of unconscious anger at your parents. However, you may have learned as a child that feeling anger at your parents is unacceptable or shameful. Thus, as an adult you must channel the anger somewhere else in order not to experience the unacceptable or shameful feelings. You might turn the anger against yourself, which may result in low self-esteem, guilt, and depression.

The third assumption is that it is helpful to learn about the roots of unconscious conflicts and allow yourself to experience these conflicts. Once these two processes have taken place, the idea is you should no longer need to spend so much emotional energy trying to avoid the conflicts. In the example above, you might gain insight into the real source of your anger, become more comfortable with it over time, and therefore no longer need to turn the anger inward. There is some evidence that short-term versions of insight-oriented therapy are effective treatments for depression (Leichsenring 2001).

Can Insight-Oriented Therapy Be Combined with Behavioral Activation?

This sort of combined approach is a bit more difficult to pull off, though not impossible. Part of the difficulty is that the two treatments originate from very different models of what depression is and how to work with it. In a behavioral approach, depression is seen as a natural response to a difficult life. The focus is on changing how you respond to difficulties in your life and how your responses positively or negatively affect your mood. In an insight-oriented approach, depression is seen as a set of symptoms caused by attempts to ward off unconscious psychological conflicts. As discussed above, change is assumed to occur when you achieve insight into the conflicts and the deep emotions associated with the conflicts surface.

These different models lead to different methods for working with depression. Insight-oriented therapies typically require you to see a therapist because it's very difficult to achieve insight into your own unconscious conflicts by yourself. In addition, from an insight-oriented perspective, it doesn't make much sense to change behavior without first understanding what's going on in your mind. On the other hand, self-activation therapy encourages you to change behavior that you associate with depression whether or not you understand its root. Which framework will work better for you depends upon a number of factors, such as

- How much do you buy the model of depression in each approach?

- Do you want to see a therapist?

- How important is it to you to understand how your childhood has affected you?

- What approaches to working with depression have been helpful to you in the past?

We want to emphasize that you do not necessarily need to use an insight-oriented approach to make sense out of the past and to see how it affects you now. Imagine, for example, that you were raised in a family where one or both of your parents struggled with depression. Research has shown that parental depression is associated with particular aspects of young children's emotional and cognitive development (Kurstjens and Wolke 2001). Thus, there is reason to suspect that your parent's depression has affected you. In order to make use of this knowledge, you do not need to understand all of your deepest feelings and conflicts about your early relationship with your parents. Instead, you can simply ask yourself such questions as, "What did I learn about how to cope with depression from my parents? How am I responding to my moods now as a function of what I learned when I was younger?" Awareness of the behavioral patterns you learned as a child might make it easier to recognize and change them in your current life.

Interpersonal Therapy

Interpersonal therapy (Klerman et al. 1984) proceeds from the assumption that relationships with others are a key factor in causing and ending depression. You may have noticed that your mood gets better or worse depending on the sorts of interactions you have with different people. Or, it could be that a particularly difficult relationship or a lack of relationships has contributed to your depression. Broadly speaking, the goal of interpersonal therapy is to strengthen your relationships with others, either by resolving conflict or strengthening existing relationships or by creating new satisfying relationships. Interpersonal therapy has been shown to be an effective treatment for depression (Elkin et al. 1989).

Can Interpersonal Therapy Be Combined with Behavioral Activation?

Like insight-oriented therapy, interpersonal therapy is usually conducted with a professional therapist's help. However, if you've noticed that parts of your self-activation approach to ending depression involve relating with others, you're probably already including aspects of an interpersonal approach. For example, many of the situations or emotions you may have been avoiding involve other people. As you activate yourself to begin ending depression, your relationships with others are likely to improve as well.

Medication

Your family doctor, a psychiatrist, or a nurse practitioner may suggest that you take medication to help your depression. The most common medications for depression are the SSRIs (selective serotonin reuptake inhibitors). These medications help increase the levels of serotonin (an important chemical neurotransmitter) available in your nervous system. A solid body of research now indicates that SSRIs, as well as some other medications, are effective treatments for depression. Studies that have compared medication to cognitive, behavioral, and interpersonal therapies have typically found no differences between the treatments in terms of their average effectiveness (Blacker 1996). One study did find a particular antidepressant medication to be superior to cognitive therapy for severely depressed patients (Elkin et al. 1989). However, this finding was not predicted and has not been replicated.

Although medication appears to be an effective treatment for depression, rates of relapse following successful treatment are consistently higher for people who discontinue medication compared to those who stay on it (Kupfer and Frank 1992). Thus, medication is not a short-term option. People often stay on medication for one to two years or even longer.

Revisiting the Concept of Chemical Imbalance

Although medications are effective treatments for depression, and levels of certain neurotransmitters in the nervous system are associated with depression, this does not mean that depression is caused by a "chemical imbalance." We discussed this in chapter 1, but it's worth emphasizing.

The idea that depression is caused by a chemical imbalance in your brain is now so common that many people believe it is an established scientific fact. If you think that a problem is caused by something biological and specific, it makes sense to assume that the only way to cure the problem is to fix or remove the biological cause (take medication). However, there are two problems with this logic: First, it is far from an established scientific fact that biological processes cause depression. Knowing that two things tend to go together (chemical imbalances and depression) does not mean that one thing causes the other. Second, there is an ample amount of scientific evidence showing that environmental events in people's lives, interpersonal issues, and negative thinking styles are all correlated with depression. So far, no one has been able to determine an exact cause of depression. Although environmental, interpersonal, and biological factors have been examined, it cannot be concluded that any of these factors, including biological, are wholly responsible for depression.

It's also a problem to assume that taking medication is the only effective treatment for depression. In fact, there are a variety of nonbiological treatments that effectively treat depression. Of course, it's possible that behavioral activation, cognitive therapy, interpersonal therapy, and psychodynamic theory all reach important biological processes through indirect means. However, even if someone someday proves that depression has a biological cause, you should be clear that there is no scientific basis for the idea that depression must be treated by medication.

Can Medication Be Combined with Behavioral Activation?

There are currently no studies examining the effects of combining antidepressant medications with self-activation therapy. However, there is some evidence that combining antidepressants with cognitive therapy produces greater effects than either treatment alone when people are severely depressed (Segal and Levitt 2002). Certainly, there is no reason to think that combining medication and self-activation would be harmful. However, research still needs to be conducted.

Our recommendation is this: Unless you are severely depressed, wait to take medication until you have given self-activation a sustained effort for at least a few weeks. Our reason for suggesting this is based on the higher rates of relapse that occur when people take medication alone and then discontinue it. Plus, many medications do have side effects that can be troublesome.

If you do choose to take medication in the context of working on self-activation, it may help to view the medication as helping you to get going in your life, rather than fixing a chemical imbalance. This perspective will help you feel more in control of the changes you are making. It will also keep you focused on learning new ways of responding to situations or feelings that can help you prevent future episodes of depression or cope better with them when they do arise.

You now understand the key ways to end depression through self-activation. We have covered the importance of links between your activities and your mood. We have also explored the various ways avoidance of feelings and situations can contribute to depression and how to get out of TRAPs by getting back on TRAC. You have also seen how activation techniques can be used to accomplish tasks and goals in life, from everyday things such as paying bills to larger issues such as finding a new job or beginning or ending a relationship. Finally, you have had a chance to reflect on what you have learned about yourself and how self-activation has or has not impacted your life. At this point, you have many options ahead. You can continue to work on self-activation, you can take a break from working on depression, you can choose an alternative approach, or you can combine self-activation with other treatments. As always, you have many choices! We wish you the best of luck in your process of building the life you want.

Appendix

Copies of Monitoring Forms

Activity-and-Mood Monitoring Chart

Before writing on the activity-and-mood monitoring chart, you should make photocopies so that you can use it again. You will use this chart in later exercises. In each box write the activities you engaged in during the hour, and how you felt. Rate your feeling on a scale of 1 to 10, with 1 being the least intensity of feeling and 10 being the most.

Time	Day and Date:
Midnight	
Mood	
1:00 A.M.	
Mood	
2:00 A.M.	
Mood	
3:00 A.M.	
Mood	
4:00 A.M.	
Mood	
5:00 A.M.	
Mood	
6:00 A.M.	
Mood	
7:00 A.M.	
Mood	
8:00 A.M.	
Mood	
9:00 A.M.	
Mood	
10:00 A.M.	
Mood	

11:00 A.M.	
Mood	
Noon	
Mood	
1:00 P.M.	
Mood	
2:00 P.M.	
Mood	
3:00 P.M.	
Mood	
4:00 P.M.	
Mood	
5:00 P.M.	
Mood	
6:00 P.M.	
Mood	
7:00 P.M.	
Mood	
8:00 P.M.	
Mood	
9:00 P.M.	
Mood	
10:00 P.M.	
Mood	
11:00 P.M.	
Mood	

TRAP Worksheet

Instructions: Fill in the blanks for four different TRAPs that you find yourself in.

TRAP 1

Circumstance: _____

Trigger: _____

Response: _____

Avoidance Pattern: _____

Consequences: _____

TRAP 2

Circumstance: _____

Trigger: _____

Response: _____

Avoidance Pattern: _____

Consequences: _____

TRAP 3

Circumstance: _____

Trigger: _____

Response: _____

Avoidance Pattern: _____

Consequences: _____

TRAP 4

Circumstance: _____

Trigger: _____

Response: _____

Avoidance Pattern: _____

Consequences: _____

What did you notice from the TRAP worksheet? Were some TRAPs easier to recognize than others? You may want to carry little TRAP cards with you that you can fill out whenever you notice a particular avoidance pattern happening. The more you can increase your awareness of TRAPs, the easier it is to get out of them, which is the next step.

TRAC Worksheet

You can make copies of this worksheet for future use. For each circumstance in which you have identified a TRAP, fill in the information that will help you get back on TRAC. Using the same circumstances, triggers, and responses from your TRAP worksheet, write down several possible alternative coping behaviors to break the avoidance pattern. Then choose one alternative and commit to a time to try it. Observe the consequences once you've tried the alternative behavior and continue to use this method with other alternatives.

TRAC

Circumstance: _____

Trigger: _____

Response: _____

Possible Alternative Coping Behaviors: _____

_____

_____

Choose One Alternative to Try: _____

_____

Commit to a time to try it: _____

Consequences: _____

References

American Psychiatric Association (APA). 1994. *Diagnostic and Statistical Manual of Mental Disorders*. 4th edition. Washington D.C.: American Psychiatric Association.

Barlow, D. H. 1988. *Anxiety and Its Disorders: The Nature and Treatment of Anxiety and Panic*. New York: Guilford Press.

Beck, A. T., A. J. Rush, B. F. Shaw, and G. Emery. 1979. *Cognitive Therapy of Depression*. New York: Guilford Press.

Blacker, D. 1996. Maintenance treatment of major depression: A review of the literature. *Harvard Review of Psychiatry* 4:1–9.

Dimidjian, S., S. Hollon, K. Dobson, K. Schmaling, B. Kohlenberg, J. McGlinchey, D. Markley, D. Atkins, M. Addis, and D. Dunner. 2003. Behavioral activation, cognitive therapy, and antidepressant medication in the treatment of major depression: Design and acute phase outcomes. Paper presented at the thirty-seventh annual convention of the Association for Advancement of Behavior Therapy, Boston, November 20, 2003.

Ehlers, C. L., E. Frank, and D. J. Kupfer. 1988. Social zeitgebers and biological rhythms: A unified approach to understanding the etiology of depression. *Archives of General Psychiatry* 45:948–952.

Elkin, I., M. T. Shea, J. T. Watkins, S. D. Imber, S. M. Sotsky, J. F. Collins, D. R. Glass, P. A. Pilkonis, W. R. Leber, and J. P. Docherty. 1989. National Institute of Mental Health Treatment of Depression Collaborative Research Program: General effectiveness of treatments. *Archives of General Psychiatry* 46(11):971–982.

Ferster, C. B. 1973. A functional analysis of depression. *American Psychologist* 28:857–870.

Gatz, M., N. L. Pederson, R. Plomin, J. R. Nesselroade, and G. E. McClearn. 1992. Importance of shared genes and shared environments for symptoms of depression in older adults. *Journal of Abnormal Psychology* 101(4):701–708.

Gloaguen, V., J. Cottraux, M. Cucherat, and I. M. Blackburn. 1998. A meta-analysis of the effects of cognitive therapy in depressed patients. *Journal of Affective Disorders* 49(1):59–72.

Hayes, S. C., and E. V. Gifford. 1997. The trouble with language: Experiential avoidance, rules, and the nature of verbal events. *Psychological Science* 8(3):170–173.

Hayes, S. C., K. D. Strosahl, and K. G. Wilson. 1999. Acceptance and Commitment Therapy: An Experiential Approach to Behavior Change. New York: Guilford Press.

Hollon, S. D., R. C. Shelton, and P. T. Loosen. 1991. Cognitive therapy and pharmacotherapy for depression. *Journal of Consulting and Clinical Psychology* 59(1):88–99.

Jacobson, N. S., K. Dobson, A. E. Fruzzetti, K. B. Schmaling, and S. Salusky. 1991. Marital therapy as a treatment for depression. *Journal of Consulting and Clinical Psychology* 59(4):547–557.

Jacobson, N. S., K. S. Dobson, P. A. Truax, M. E. Addis, K. Koerner, J. K. Gollan, E. Gortner, and S. E. Prince. 1996. A component analysis of cognitive behavioral treatment for depression. *Journal of Consulting and Clinical Psychology* 64:295–304.

Klerman, G. L., M. M. Weissman, B. J. Rounsaville, and E. S. Chevron. 1984. *Interpersonal Psychotherapy of Depression*. New York: Basic Books.

Kupfer, D. J., and E. Frank. 1992. The minimum length of treatment for recovery. In *Long-Term Treatment of Depression*, edited by S. A. Montgomery and F. Roulillon. New York: Wiley.

Kurstjens, S., and D. Wolke. 2001. Effects of maternal depression on cognitive development of children over the first seven years of life. *Journal of Child Psychology and Psychiatry and Allied Disciplines* 42(5):623–636.

Laird, J. D. 1974. Self-attribution of emotion: The effects of expressive behavior on the quality of emotional experience. *Journal of Personality and Social Psychology* 29(4):521–533.

Laird, J. D., and C. Bresler. 1992. The process of emotional experience: A self-perception theory. In *Emotion*, edited by M. S. Clark. Thousand Oaks, Calif.: Sage.

Leichsenring, F. 2001. Comparative effects of short-term psychodynamic psychotherapy and cognitive-behavioral therapy in depression: A meta-analytic approach. *Clinical Psychology Review* 21(3):401–419.

Lewinsohn, P. M. 1974. A behavioral approach to depression. In *The Psychology of Depression: Contemporary Theory and Research*, edited by R. J. Friedman and M. M. Katz. Washington, D.C.: Winston-Wiley.

Lyubomirsky, S., and S. Nolen-Hoeksema. 1995. Effects of self-focused rumination on negative thinking and interpersonal problem solving. *Journal of Personality and Social Psychology* 69(1):176–190.

Lyubomirsky, S., and C. Tkach. 2003. The consequences of dysphoric rumination. In *Depressive Rumination: Nature, Theory, and Treatment*, edited by C. Papageorgiou and A. Wells. Chichester, U.K.: Wiley.

Lyubomirsky, S., K. L. Tucker, N. D. Caldwell, and K. Berg. 1999. Why ruminators are poor problems solvers: Clues from the phenomenology of dysphoric rumination. *Journal of Personality and Social Psychology* 77:1041–1060.

Martell, C. R., M. E. Addis, and N. S. Jacobson. 2001. *Depression in Context: Strategies for Guided Action.* New York: W. W. Norton.

Nesse, R. M. 2000. Is depression an adaptation? *Archives of General Psychiatry* 57:1–20.

Nolen-Hoeksema, S., L. E. Parker, and J. Larson. 1994. Ruminative coping with depressed mood following loss. *Journal of Personality and Social Psychology* 67(1):92–104.

Norcross, J. C., and D. J. Vangarelli. 1988. The resolution solution: Longitudinal examination of New Year's change attempts. *Journal of Substance Abuse* 1:127–134.

Papageorgiou, C., and A. Wells. 2003. An empirical test of a clinical metacognitive model of rumination and depression. *Cognitive Therapy and Research* 27:261–273.

Pyszczynski, T., and J. Greenberg. 1987. Self-regulatory perseveration and the depressive self-focusing style: A self-awareness theory of reactive depression. *Psychological Bulletin* 201: 122–138.

Schlenker, B. R., D. W. Dlugolecki, and K. Doherty. 1994. The impact of self-presentations on self-appraisals and behavior: The power of public commitment. *Personality and Social Psychology Bulletin* 20(1):20–33.

Scogin, F., J. Bynum, G. Stephens, and S. Calhoon. 1990. Efficacy of self-administered treatment programs: Meta-analytic review. *Professional Psychology: Research and Practice* 21(1):42–47.

Segal, Z., and V. P. Levitt. 2002. Efficacy of combined, sequential, and crossover psychotherapy and pharmacotherapy in improving outcomes in depression. *Journal of Psychiatry and Neuroscience* 27(4):281–290.

Seligman, M. E. P. 1995. The effectiveness of psychotherapy: The Consumer Reports study. *American Psychologist* 50(12):965–974.

Strack, F., L. Martin, and S. Stepper. 1988. Inhibiting and facilitating conditions of the human smile: A non-obtrusive test of the facial feedback hypothesis. *Journal of Personality and Social Psychology* 54(5):768–777.

Teasdale, J. D., Z. V. Segal, J. M. G. Williams, V. A. Ridgeway, J. M. Soulsby, and M. A. Lau. 2000. Prevention of relapse/recurrence in major depression by mindfulness-based cognitive therapy. *Journal of Consulting and Clinical Psychology* 68(4):615–623.

Wells, A., and K. Carter. 2001. Further tests of a cognitive model of generalized anxiety disorder: Metacognitions and worry in GAD, panic disorder, social phobia, depression, and non-patients. *U.S. Association for the Advancement of Behavior Therapy* 31(1):85–102.

Wolpe, J., and A. A. Lazarus. 1966. *Behavior Therapy Techniques.* New York: Pergamon Press.

Michael E. Addis, Ph.D., is associate professor of psychology at Clark University in Worcester, MA. For several years, he has served as a clinical supervisor and trainer of therapists conducting behavioral activation treatments for depression. He received his BA from the University of California, Berkeley, in 1987, and his Ph.D. from the University of Washington in 1995. He has published over forty scientific articles and books on a range of topics including the treatment of depression, the relationship between research and practice in clinical psychology, and men's mental health. He is past recipient of the President's New Researcher Award from the Association for the Advancement of Behavior Therapy. In 2003, He received the researcher of the year award from the Society for the Psychological Study of Men and Masculinity, and the American Psychological Association's David Shakow Award for early career contributions to the science and practice of clinical psychology

Christopher R. Martell, Ph.D., ABPP is clinical associate professor of psychology at the University of Washington in Seattle, WA, where he also maintains a private practice. He is board certified in clinical psychology and behavioral psychology by the American Board of Professional Psychology and is a founding fellow of the Academy of Cognitive Therapy. He is first author of the books *Depression in Context: Strategies for Guided Action* and *Cognitive Behavioral Therapies with Lesbian, Gay, and Bisexual Clients*. He has published articles and book chapters on behavioral treatments for depression, couples therapy, and issues affecting gay, lesbian and bisexual individuals. He is past president of the Washington State Psychological Association. He has conducted professional workshops on behavioral activation treatment for depression in the U.S. and Internationally.

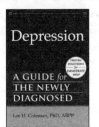

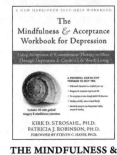
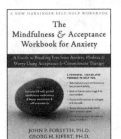
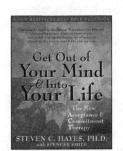

FROM OUR PUBLISHER—

As the publisher at New Harbinger and a clinical psychologist since 1978, I know that emotional problems are best helped with evidence-based therapies. These are the treatments derived from scientific research (randomized controlled trials) that show what works. Whether these treatments are delivered by trained clinicians or found in a self-help book, they are designed to provide you with proven strategies to overcome your problem.

Therapies that aren't evidence-based—whether offered by clinicians or in books—are much less likely to help. In fact, therapies that aren't guided by science may not help you at all. That's why this New Harbinger book is based on scientific evidence that the treatment can relieve emotional pain.

This is important: if this book isn't enough, and you need the help of a skilled therapist, use the following resources to find a clinician trained in the evidence-based protocols appropriate for your problem. And if you need more support—a community that understands what you're going through and can show you ways to cope—resources for that are provided below, as well.

Real help is available for the problems you have been struggling with. The skills you can learn from evidence-based therapies will change your life.

Matthew McKay, PhD
Publisher, New Harbinger Publications

new harbinger
CELEBRATING
40 YEARS

**If you need a therapist, the following organization
can help you find a therapist trained in cognitive behavioral therapy (CBT).**

The Association for Behavioral & Cognitive Therapies (ABCT) Find-a-Therapist service offers a list of therapists schooled in CBT techniques. Therapists listed are licensed professionals who have met the membership requirements of ABCT and who have chosen to appear in the directory.
Please visit www.abct.org and click on *Find a Therapist*.

**For additional support for patients, family, and friends,
please contact the following:**

Anxiety and Depression Association of American (ADAA)
Please visit www.adaa.org

Depression and Bipolar Support Alliance (DBSA)
Visit www.dbsalliance.org

National Alliance on Mental Illness (NAMI)
Please visit www.nami.org